D1568793

Mama D's Old-Fashioned Italian Cooking

OTHER BOOKS BY GIOVANNA D'AGOSTINO

Mama D's Italian-Style Cooking
Mama D's Italian Cooking with a Pinch
Pasta & Pizza

Mama D's Old-Fashioned Italian Cooking

Giovanna D'Agostino

Prentice Hall Press

New York London Toronto Sydney Tokyo

Prentice Hall Press
Gulf+Western Building
One Gulf+Western Plaza
New York, New York 10023

PRENTICE HALL PRESS and colophon are registered
trademarks of Simon & Schuster, Inc.

Library of Congress Cataloging-in-Publication Data

D'Agostino, Giovanna.
Mama D's old-fashioned Italian cooking.
Includes index.
1. Cookery, Italian.   I. Title.
TX723.D254   1989   641.5945   88-12623
ISBN 0-13-548132-5

Manufactured in the United States of America

10 9 8 7 6 5 4 3 2 1

First Edition

*This book is dedicated to
Maria Giuesseppe, my Mama,
for the love and care she gave me
and for always being there to correct me
when I needed it*

ACKNOWLEDGMENTS

I want to thank the many dear Italian ladies who taught me how to cook when I was a young married woman, when I was trying to learn how. Also, I want to express my thanks to my former landlady, Mrs. Roy Cinquegrani, who really taught me how to cook "with a pinch of this and a pinch of that." And I will always be indebted to my two sisters-in-law, Rosina and Felicia, who were such excellent cooks and who made me want to stay for supper whenever I visited their homes in Chicago. I not only learned their ways of cooking, but also the various Italian dialects. When I eventually visited Italy in the summer of 1970, I found that I had much to be grateful for—from my many friends in both Chicago and Minneapolis.

Contents

Soups

Stracciatella Soup

3 cups water
2 tablespoons butter
2 eggs
2 teaspoons fine semolina
2 tablespoons freshly grated
   Romano cheese
1 teaspoon salt
½ teaspoon freshly ground
   black pepper

Heat the water and butter. Let the mixture cool to room temperature. Beat the eggs and blend with the semolina and cheese. Add 1 cup of the butter-water broth and beat well. Bring the remaining broth to a boil and slowly add the egg mixture, beating it into the broth with a fork. Add the salt and pepper. Cook for 4 or 5 minutes over medium heat. Serve hot.

Serves 4.

Buy your Parmesan and Romano cheese in chunks and grate it yourself. You never know how long ago the grated cheese in cans or jars was packed. Often it's dry and all the flavor is gone. Grate your cheese as you need it. Wrap it in a damp cloth and before storing it in your refrigerator. If the cloth is kept moist, your cheese will not dry out.

Minestrone

1 pound dried white beans
   (great northern or other
   white beans)
4 stalks celery, sliced
4 carrots, diced
2 potatoes, peeled and diced
½ cup chopped parsley
1 16-ounce can chickpeas,
   drained
   Salt and freshly ground black
   pepper to taste
½ cup oil
2 onions, diced
4 cloves garlic, minced
   Salt and freshly ground black
   pepper to taste
3 or 4 ripe tomatoes, chopped
1 medium zucchini, diced

Fill a 6- to 8-quart stockpot with water to about 4 inches from the top. Wash the beans thoroughly, put them in the stockpot, and cook until just tender, about 30 to 40 minutes. Replace the water lost in cooking and return to a boil. Add the celery, carrots, potatoes, 2 tablespoons of the chopped parsley, chickpeas, salt, and pepper.

Heat the oil in a small saucepan. Add the onions, garlic, the remaining chopped parsley, additional salt and pepper to taste, and sauté until the onions are golden brown. Add the tomatoes and cook for 20 to 30 minutes over medium-low heat. Add the mixture to the beans and vegetables and cook slowly for 1 hour more. Add the zucchini for the final 20 minutes of cooking.

Serves 20 or more.

N O T E : Freeze any leftover soup for future meals.

Minestrone, Tuscan Style

1 pound dried great northern
  beans
4 quarts water
½ cup oil
2 onions, coarsely chopped
4 cloves garlic, minced
2 tablespoons chopped fresh
  parsley
½ teaspoon salt
¼ teaspoon freshly ground
  black pepper
3 or 4 ripe tomatoes, coarsley
  chopped
4 stalks celery, sliced
4 carrots, diced
2 medium potatoes, peeled and
  diced
1 16-ounce can chickpeas
1 tablespoon chopped fresh
  parsley
1 tablespoon salt
¼ teaspoon freshly ground
  black pepper
1 medium zucchini, diced
1 cup maruzzine

Thoroughly wash the beans. Put the beans and water in a stockpot and cook the beans until just tender, about 30 to 40 minutes.

While the beans are cooking, heat the oil in a heavy 8-inch skillet over medium heat. Add the onions, garlic, 2 tablespoons chopped parsley, ½ teaspoon salt, and ¼ teaspoon pepper. Cook, stirring, until the onions are golden brown. Reduce the heat to medium-low, add the tomatoes, and cook, uncovered, for about 20 to 30 minutes or until the tomatoes are reduced.

Replace the water lost in the bean pot during the cooking and add the tomato mixture along with the celery, carrots, potatoes, chickpeas with their liquid, and the 1 tablespoon chopped parsley, 1 tablespoon salt, and ¼ teaspoon pepper. Simmer, covered, for 1 hour.

About 10 minutes before the end of the cooking time, bring the soup to a boil. Add the zucchini and pasta. Cook until the pasta is al dente.

Serves 8 to 10.

Minestrone with Ground Beef

¼ cup vegetable oil
1 pound ground beef
2 medium onions, minced
2 cloves garlic, minced
2 tablespoons minced parsley
1 16-ounce can tomatoes, or 6
  fresh tomatoes, crushed
4 quarts water
2 stalks celery, diced
2 carrots, peeled and diced
2 potatoes, peeled and sliced
½ pound fresh or frozen peas
½ pound green beans
½ cup freshly grated Romano
  cheese

Heat the oil in a large saucepan. Add the meat, onions, garlic, and parsley. Sauté until the meat is lightly browned. Add the tomatoes and cook for 10 minutes over low heat. Put the water in a 6-quart stockpot and bring to a boil. Add the celery, carrots, and potatoes. Add the tomato mixture and simmer for 1 hour. Add the peas and beans and simmer for an additional hour. Ladle the soup into bowls and top each with cheese.

Serves 6.

Broccoli Soup with Tubettini

½ pound salt pork, diced
1½ tablespoons vegetable oil
1½ tablespoons olive oil
2 onions, finely chopped
2 cloves garlic, minced
1 6-ounce can tomato paste
3 quarts water
1 teaspoon salt
¼ teaspoon freshly ground black pepper
1 10-ounce package frozen broccoli, or 3 stems fresh broccoli
1 cup tubettini
½ cup freshly grated Romano cheese

Brown the salt pork in a heavy 4-quart pot over medium heat. Drain the fat and add the oils, onions, garlic, tomato paste, water, salt, and pepper. Bring to a boil and cook for 25 minutes. Add the broccoli and pasta and cook for 10 minutes more. Serve in bowls while hot and sprinkle each serving with Romano cheese.

Serves 6.

Spinach and Bean Minestra

4 tablespoons vegetable or olive oil
½ pound bacon, diced
3 cloves garlic, minced
1 pound spinach, cooked, drained, and chopped (reserve 2 cups of the cooking water)
1 teaspoon salt
¼ teaspoon freshly ground black pepper
¼ teaspoon dried oregano leaves
1 cup ditalini, cooked and rinsed in cold water
1 20-ounce can cannellini or other white beans
1 quart water
½ cup freshly grated Romano cheese

Heat the oil in a heavy pot over medium heat. Cook the bacon until it is done but not crisp. Pour off all but about 6 tablespoons of the fat. Add the garlic. Cook, stirring, until the garlic is golden. Add the spinach and its cooking water, the salt, pepper, oregano, ditalini, cannellini, and 1 quart water. Stir over low heat for 5 minutes. Stir in the Romano cheese and serve.

Serves 4.

N O T E : Minestra is a very thick soup, almost a stew.

Bean and Bacon Soup

- 1 pound great northern beans
- 4 quarts water
- 2 tablespoons olive or vegetable oil
- 2 medium onions, finely chopped
- 2 cloves garlic, minced
- ½ pound bacon, cut into small pieces
- ¼ teaspoon freshly ground black pepper
- ¼ teaspoon dried oregano leaves
- 1 teaspoon dried basil leaves
- 2 tablespoons chopped fresh parsley
- 1 tablespoon salt
- 2 medium potatoes, peeled and diced
- 3 stalks celery, chopped
- 3 carrots, sliced
- 1 cup tubettini, cooked al dente and rinsed in cold water
  Freshly grated Romano cheese

Wash the beans thoroughly, put them in a bowl, and add water to cover the beans by a few inches; soak overnight.

Put the beans and their soaking water into a 6- to 8-quart pot. Add the water and bring to a boil. Lower the heat and simmer the beans, covered, for 1 hour.

While the beans are cooking, heat the oil in a heavy 8-inch skillet over medium heat. Add the onions, garlic, and bacon, and cook, stirring, until the onions are transparent. Add the pepper, oregano, basil, and parsley.

Replace the water lost in the bean pot during cooking, and add the salt, potatoes, celery, and carrots. Bring the liquid to a boil. Add the onion mixture. Reduce the heat and simmer, partially covered, for 2 hours.

Add the cooked pasta and simmer for 2 to 3 minutes. Serve the soup while still very hot in large bowls and sprinkle each serving with grated cheese.

Serves 8 to 10.

Clam Soup

- 2 tablespoons vegetable or olive oil
- 2 cloves garlic, minced
- 1 onion, chopped
- ½ cup dry white wine
- 4 cups coarsely chopped tomatoes
- 3 tablespoons minced fresh parsley
- 2 cups canned chopped clams, undrained
- 1 teaspoon salt
- ¼ teaspoon freshly ground black pepper
- ¼ cup freshly grated Parmesan cheese
- 8 cups boiling water

Heat the oil in a 4- to 6-quart saucepan. Add the garlic and onion and sauté until the onion is transparent. Add the wine, tomatoes, parsley, clams, salt, and pepper. Simmer, covered, for 20 minutes. Add the cheese and water and simmer, uncovered, for 45 minutes. Serve hot.

Serves 4 to 6.

Spring Soup

2 tablespoons butter
2 tablespoons vegetable or olive oil
1 small onion, chopped
2 cloves garlic, minced
2 tablespoons chopped fresh parsley
4 ripe tomatoes, seeded and chopped
1½ teaspoons salt
¼ teaspoon freshly ground black pepper
¼ teaspoon dried oregano leaves
2 quarts beef or Chicken Broth (see page 40)
2 stalks celery, sliced
2 medium zucchini, sliced
2 carrots, sliced
2 potatoes, peeled and diced
1 10-ounce package frozen artichoke hearts, thawed and cut into chunks
1 pound fresh or frozen peas
1 pound orzo, cooked and rinsed in cold water
½ cup freshly grated Romano cheese

Melt the butter in the oil in a heavy skillet or saucepan over medium heat. Add the onion, garlic, and parsley. Cook, stirring, until the onion is transparent. Add the tomatoes, salt, pepper, and oregano. Lower the heat and simmer for about 15 minutes.

Heat the stock to a boil in a large pot. Add the remaining vegetables and the tomato mixture from the skillet. Cook slowly, covered, for 20 minutes or until the vegetables are tender. Add the pasta and stir in the grated cheese until thoroughly mixed.

Serves 8.

Salads & Antipasti

Fontina Fondue Italiano

3 ½ cups milk
1 ½ pounds fontina cheese,
   coarsely grated
   5 tablespoons all-purpose
   flour
   2 cloves garlic, minced
   1 teaspoon salt
   ⅛ teaspoon freshly ground
   black pepper
   ¼ cup kirsch
   French Bread Crusts (recipe
   follows)

Bring the milk to a boil in the top of a double boiler. Shake the grated cheese in a paper bag with the flour, garlic, salt, and pepper. Add a handful of the cheese mixture at a time to the boiling milk and stir until it is all combined. Add the kirsch and stir well. Pour the mixture into a fondue pot or oven warmer. Keep it hot while guests help themselves by dipping the French Bread Crusts into the fondue.

Serves 4.

French Bread Crusts

3 eggs
1 tablespoon freshly grated
   Parmesan cheese
1 teaspoon salt
¼ teaspoon freshly ground
   black pepper
1 clove garlic, minced
8 slices of bread with crusts
   (preferably French bread)
¼ cup oil

Beat the eggs with the cheese, salt, pepper, and garlic. Mix well. Cut the bread into 1-inch cubes. Dip the cubes in the egg mixture. Heat the oil in an 8-inch skillet. Fry the bread cubes in the skillet until all sides are golden brown. Serve with fondue.

Mozzarella in Carrozza

3 eggs
½ teaspoon salt
¼ teaspoon freshly ground
   black pepper
1 teaspoon minced garlic
3 tablespoons minced fresh
   parsley
4 slices bread
4 slices mozzarella cheese
¼ cup freshly grated Romano
   cheese

Preheat the broiler.
   Beat the eggs with the salt, pepper, garlic, and parsley. Dip the slices of bread into the egg mixture and place on a greased cookie sheet. Dip the mozzarella slices in the egg mixture and place one slice on each piece of bread. Sprinkle the Romano cheese over the top of each slice. Broil until the mozzarella is melted. Serve hot.

Serves 4.

Quattro Bean Salad

1 cup cooked green beans
1 cup cooked yellow wax beans
1 cup kidney beans
1 cup chickpeas
1 onion, sliced in rings
1 green pepper, cut in thin
   rings
½ teaspoon freshly ground
   black pepper
1 teaspoon salt
½ cup sugar
1 teaspoon minced garlic
⅓ cup olive oil
⅓ cup wine vinegar

Gently toss all ingredients together in a bowl and serve.

Serves 4 to 6.

Celery, Carrot, and Raisin Salad

1½ cups raisins
1½ cups diced celery
1 cup grated carrots
½ teaspoon salt
  Juice of 1 lemon
4 lettuce leaves

Soften the raisins in hot water and drain. When cool, place the raisins in a bowl with the celery and carrots. Season with salt. Pour the lemon juice over the salad. Serve on lettuce leaves.

Serves 4.

Fontina Cheese and Pepper Salad

3 green peppers, diced
8 ounces fontina cheese, diced
½ cup whole green Italian
   olives
½ cup black olives
1 clove garlic, minced
   Pinch of salt
½ teaspoon freshly ground
   black pepper
¼ cup olive oil
1 tablespoon wine vinegar
1 tablespoon freshly grated
   Romano cheese

Mix together the green peppers, cheese, olives, and garlic. Season with salt and pepper. In a covered container, shake the oil and vinegar to combine. Drizzle the dressing over the salad; toss gently. Sprinkle with Romano cheese.

Serves 4.

Lentil Salad

1 cup lentils
3 small onions, finely chopped
1 small bay leaf
2 stalks celery, diced
3 tablespoons chopped fresh parsley
3 small tomatoes, quartered
1 tablespoon wine vinegar
5 tablespoons olive oil
¼ teaspoon freshly ground black pepper
1 clove garlic, minced
Salt, to taste
Romano or Parmesan cheese, grated

Put the lentils, ⅓ of the onions, and the bay leaf in a saucepan. Add water to cover and simmer until the lentils are tender, about 45 minutes. Drain, and discard the bay leaf. When cooled, put the lentil mixture in a salad bowl. Add the remaining ingredients and toss gently to combine.

Serves 4 to 6.

Neapolitan Salad

2 cups cooked cauliflower florets
2 tablespoons chopped anchovy fillets
2 tablespoons drained capers
12 black olives
½ cup chopped celery
1 small onion, chopped
1 teaspoon salt
¼ teaspoon freshly ground black pepper
2 cloves garlic, minced
3 tablespoons oil
1 tablespoon wine vinegar
¼ cup freshly grated Romano cheese

Put cauliflower, anchovies, capers, olives, celery, and onion in a bowl. Season with salt, pepper, and garlic. Drizzle the oil and vinegar over the salad and toss gently. Sprinkle the salad with Romano cheese and serve.

Serves 4.

Chickpea Salad

       1 20-ounce can chickpeas,
          drained
       3 green peppers, diced
      10 pimento-stuffed green olives
       1 small onion, diced
       2 to 3 tablespoons drained
          capers
       2 tablespoons wine vinegar
       6 tablespoons olive oil
       1 teaspoon salt
     ¼ teaspoon freshly ground
          black pepper
       1 clove garlic, minced

Mix all ingredients together and marinate in the refrigerator for several hours until ready to serve.

Serves 4 to 6.

Italian-Style Cabbage Salad

       1 small head cabbage,
          shredded
       2 medium carrots, shredded
       1 onion, minced
       2 stalks celery, diced
     ½ teaspoon sugar
     ½ teaspoon salt
     ¼ teaspoon freshly ground
          black pepper
     ½ teaspoon minced garlic
       6 tablespoons olive oil
       2 tablespoons wine vinegar

Put the cabbage, carrots, onion, and celery in a bowl. Add the sugar, salt, pepper, and garlic. Drizzle the oil and vinegar over the salad and toss to combine.

Serves 4 to 6.

Onion Salad

       2 large onions
       1 tablespoon salt
     ½ teaspoon freshly ground
          black pepper
     ¼ cup olive oil
       3 tablespoons lemon juice

Boil the onions in a 2-quart saucepan with enough water to cover until they are tender, about 5 minutes. Cool and slice. Put the onions on a platter and season with salt and pepper. Mix the oil and lemon juice. Pour over the onion slices and serve.

Serves 4.

Potato, Chicory, and Egg Salad

6 peeled, boiled potatoes
1 small head chicory
4 hard-boiled eggs, peeled and diced
1 teaspoon minced garlic
¼ teaspoon freshly ground black pepper
4 tablespoons olive oil
1 tablespoon vinegar

Dice the potatoes into a salad bowl. Tear the chicory into bite-size pieces and add to the potatoes along with the eggs. Add the garlic and pepper. Drizzle with the oil and vinegar and toss gently. Serve either warm or cold.

Serves 4.

When you're making salads, *drizzle* the oil on. Don't *pour* it or it will just run to the bottom of the bowl—what good is that? If you're using tomatoes in your salad, you don't really need vinegar. The tomato has enough acid; all you need is the oil and herbs.

Always season your lettuce with herbs before you add the oil. For a really flavorful salad, put the seasonings on the lettuce and let the lettuce stand in the refrigerator for two or three hours before serving. When you add the herbs to the salad dressing, the oil coats the spices and you don't get all of the flavor.

Eggplant Caponatina

2 small eggplants
Salt as needed
¼ cup olive oil
1 small stalk celery, with leaves, chopped
2 small onions, chopped
½ cup vinegar
5 teaspoons sugar
1 29-ounce can plum tomatoes, drained
10 green olives, pitted and slivered
1 3½-ounce bottle capers, drained
1 2-ounce can anchovy fillets
1 teaspoon salt
¼ teaspoon freshly ground black pepper

Pare the eggplants and cut them into ½-inch cubes. Salt generously and drain in a colander for about 15 minutes.

Heat the olive oil in a large skillet. Add the celery and cook for 10 minutes. Add the onions and sauté until the onions are soft and lightly colored. Transfer the celery and onions to a bowl with a slotted spoon. Transfer the eggplant to the skillet and sauté until lightly browned, about 10 minutes.

In a small bowl, mix the vinegar and sugar. Return the celery and onions to the skillet and stir in the vinegar and sugar, tomatoes, olives, capers, anchovies, 1 teaspoon salt, and pepper. Bring to a boil, reduce heat, and simmer, uncovered, for 20 minutes. If necessary, add a little more vinegar. Simmer the mixture a few more minutes. Put it in a serving bowl and refrigerate, covered, until ready to serve.

Serves 6 to 8.

Chicken Spread Italiano

        2   cups cooked, minced chicken
      ½   teaspoon minced garlic
      ⅛   teaspoon dried oregano
      ½   cup diced celery
      ¼   cup chopped pimento-stuffed
            olives
        1   teaspoon mustard
        1   cup mayonnaise
        2   tablespoons minced parsley
            Toast points

Combine all ingredients except toast and mix thoroughly. Chill well. Spread mixture on toast points and serve.

Serves 4.

Green Beans with Tuna

        1   pound fresh green beans,
            cleaned
      ¼   cup vegetable or olive oil
        1   teaspoon salt
      ¼   teaspoon freshly ground
            black pepper
      ¼   teaspoon dried oregano
        2   cloves garlic, minced
        1   7-ounce can tuna, drained
            and flaked
        3   hard-boiled eggs, peeled and
            halved lengthwise
      ¼   cup freshly grated Romano
            cheese
        1   teaspoon lemon juice

Cook the beans in salted water for about 2 minutes; drain. Place the beans in a bowl. Add the oil, salt, pepper, oregano, and garlic; toss together lightly. Place the beans on a serving platter. Spoon the tuna over the beans. Garnish with the eggs. Sprinkle the cheese over all; drizzle the lemon juice over the salad and serve.

Serves 4.

NOTE: You may add 12 halved black olives and 1 finely chopped onion to make a piquant salad.

Tuna with Beans

        4   tablespoons olive oil
        2   tablespoons lemon juice
        1   teaspoon salt
      ¼   teaspoon freshly ground
            black pepper
        2   stalks celery, minced
        1   medium onion, minced
        2   cloves garlic, minced
    2½   cups great northern beans,
            drained
        1   7-ounce can tuna, drained
            and flaked
      ¼   cup freshly grated Romano
            cheese
        2   teaspoons chopped fresh
            parsley

In a large serving bowl, combine the oil, lemon juice, salt, and pepper. Add the celery, onion, garlic, beans, and tuna. Mix well. Sprinkle with cheese and parsley.

Serves 4.

Orange Salad

....

    5 oranges, peeled, seeded, and
      diced
    1 cup raisins
 1/2 teaspoon freshly ground
      black pepper
    6 tablespoons olive oil
 1/4 cup chopped walnuts
    1 head lettuce, washed and
      shredded

Place the diced oranges and raisins in a bowl. Add the pepper, oil, and walnuts. Mix together and refrigerate. To serve, arrange the salad on 4 small, lettuce-lined plates.

Serves 4.

Ricotta Cheese Salad in Tomato

....

    3 large tomatoes
    3 cups ricotta cheese
    1 onion, minced
    2 carrots, finely grated
    2 cloves garlic, minced
    3 tablespoons olive oil
    1 teaspoon white vinegar
 1/4 teaspoon freshly ground
      black pepper
    1 teaspoon salt
      Crisp lettuce leaves
    3 radishes, grated
      Chopped fresh parsley

Cut the tomatoes in half crosswise; scoop out and reserve the pulp and seeds and drain well. Put the pulp and seeds in a bowl with the ricotta cheese, onion, carrots, and garlic; mix well. Combine the oil, vinegar, pepper, and salt. Pour the dressing over the salad; toss to combine. Spoon the mixture into the tomato shells. Line the serving plate with lettuce leaves and place the tomatoes on top. Surround the tomatoes with the radishes. Sprinkle the parsley over all.

Serves 6.

Pickled Pepper Salad

....

    2 cups sliced or diced green
      and red peppers
    1 cup chopped celery
 1/2 cup Italian green or black
      olives
    1 2-ounce can anchovy fillets,
      drained, or 2 tablespoons
      capers
      Salt and freshly ground black
      pepper to taste
    1 clove garlic, crushed
    3 tablespoons olive oil
    1 tablespoon wine vinegar

Put the peppers, celery, olives, anchovies, salt, pepper, and garlic into a serving bowl. Add the oil and vinegar and toss lightly.

Serves 4.

Olive and Eggplant Salad

1 large eggplant, peeled and diced
1 small onion, chopped
  Pinch of salt
½ teaspoon freshly ground
  black pepper
1 clove garlic, minced
¼ pound black Italian olives
2 tomatoes, cut into wedges
3 sprigs parsley, chopped
¼ cup olive oil
1 tablespoon plus 1 teaspoon
  wine vinegar

Cook the eggplant in boiling, salted water until tender. Drain and remove excess water by pressing the eggplant against the side of a colander with a spoon. Combine with the remaining ingredients in a large bowl and toss gently.

Serves 4.

Zucchini and Anchovy Salad

6 small zucchini
2 small onions, thinly sliced
1 2-ounce can anchovy fillets,
  drained and mashed
  Pinch of salt
¼ teaspoon freshly ground
  black pepper
1 clove garlic, minced
2 tablespoon wine vinegar
½ cup olive oil
1 tablespoon freshly grated
  Romano cheese

Cook the zucchini in boiling water until barely tender, about 5 minutes. Drain and cut the zucchini into ½-inch-thick slices. Put the slices in a bowl and add the onions, anchovies, salt, pepper, and garlic; toss to combine. Mix the vinegar and oil and sprinkle the dressing over the salad. Sprinkle the cheese on top.

Serves 4 to 6.

Italian Anchovy Salad

1 head lettuce, chopped
1 teaspoon salt
¼ teaspoon freshly ground
  black pepper
⅛ teaspoon dried oregano
1 clove garlic, minced
1 2-ounce can anchovy fillets,
  drained and cut into pieces
1 small onion, finely chopped
5 tablespoons olive oil
1 tablespoon vinegar
1 tablespoon freshly grated
  Parmesan cheese

Place the lettuce in a salad bowl. Sprinkle on the salt, pepper, oregano, and garlic. Add the anchovies and onion. In a small covered jar, shake the oil and vinegar to combine and drizzle over the salad; toss lightly. Sprinkle with the cheese.

Serves 4 to 6.

Tuna and Vegetable Salad

½ head lettuce, cut into chunks
1 7-ounce can tuna, drained
   and flaked
1 small cucumber, thinly sliced
2 or 3 stalks celery, with
   leaves, sliced
1 clove garlic, minced
1 small onion, chopped
   Salt and freshly ground black
   pepper to taste
3 tablespoons olive oil
1 tablespoon wine vinegar
   Juice of ½ lemon
1 tablespoon grated Parmesan
   cheese

Place the lettuce, tuna, cucumber, celery, garlic, onion, salt, and pepper in a bowl and toss. In a small covered jar, shake the oil and vinegar well. Drizzle the dressing and lemon juice over the salad. Sprinkle the cheese on top. Add seasoning to taste.

Serves 4 to 6.

Artichoke-Olive Salad

1 14-ounce can artichoke
   hearts, drained
12 pitted black olives
2 teaspoons drained capers
1 2-ounce can anchovy fillets,
   drained and chopped
2 stalks celery, chopped
1 4-ounce jar pimentos,
   drained and chopped

2 hard-boiled eggs, peeled and
   sliced
1 small onion, minced
1 clove garlic, minced
¼ teaspoon freshly ground
   black pepper
1 teaspoon lemon juice
1 tablespoon wine vinegar
¼ cup olive oil

Put all the ingredients in a bowl and toss. Add seasoning to taste. Serve at room temperature.

Serves 4.

Insalata Mista

2 cups cooked string beans
1 medium onion, thinly sliced
1 cup cubed mozzarella cheese
½ cup thinly sliced pepperoni
2 cloves garlic, minced
1 teaspoon salt
¼ teaspoon freshly ground
   black pepper
4 tablespoons olive oil
1½ tablespoons wine vinegar
¼ cup freshly grated Romano
   cheese

Place the string beans, onion, mozzarella, pepperoni, and garlic in a salad bowl. Season with the salt and pepper. Toss lightly. Combine the oil and vinegar. Pour the dressing over the salad. Sprinkle the Romano cheese on top.

Serves 4.

Baccalà Salad

    1 pound baccalà (codfish),
        cleaned
    ¾ teaspoon salt
    ¼ teaspoon freshly ground
        black pepper
    2 cloves garlic, minced
    8 large green olives
    1 small onion, minced
    1 red or green pepper, julienned
        Juice of ½ lemon
    ¼ cup olive oil
    1 tablespoon vinegar

Boil the fish in a large pot of water until flaky
and tender; drain. Flake the fish, place it in a
salad bowl, and season with the salt, pepper,
and garlic. Add the olives, onion, and red or
green pepper. Squeeze the lemon juice over
the salad and sprinkle it with the oil and vinegar. Toss lightly.

Serves 4.

Warm Spinach Salad

    ¼ cup vegetable oil
    ½ pound bacon, cut in small pieces
    2 cloves garlic, minced
        Juice of 1 lemon
    1 pound spinach
    1 teaspoon salt
    ¼ teaspoon freshly ground
        black pepper
    1 medium onion, sliced in rings
    2 hard-boiled eggs, peeled and
        quartered

Heat the oil in a large skillet and fry the bacon
until crisp. Add the garlic and lemon juice.
Keep the bacon warm over low heat. Wash the
spinach thoroughly, tear it into bite-size
pieces, and put the pieces in a salad bowl.
Season with the salt and pepper. Pour the
bacon and oil over the salad, and garnish it
with the onion rings and eggs.

Serves 4.

Spinach Salad

    1 pound fresh spinach
    3 hard-boiled eggs, peeled
    1 small onion, finely chopped
    ¼ teaspoon salt
    ¼ teaspoon freshly ground
        black pepper
    2 cloves garlic, minced
    8 tablespoons olive oil
    2 tablespoons wine vinegar
    1 large tomato, cut in wedges
    2 tablespoons freshly grated
        Romano cheese

Wash the spinach thoroughly and tear into
bite-size pieces in a serving bowl. Cut the eggs
into wedges and add to the spinach along with
the onion, salt, pepper, and garlic. In a covered container, shake the oil and vinegar to
combine. Drizzle the dressing over the salad.
Garnish with the tomato wedges and sprinkle
with the Romano cheese.

Serves 4 to 6.

Cauliflower Salad

1 medium head cauliflower
1 teaspoon salt
¼ teaspoon freshly ground
black pepper
1 clove garlic, minced
2 cups diced celery
6 tablespoons vegetable oil
2 tablespoons wine vinegar
2 tablespoons capers
5 anchovy fillets, drained and
chopped
10 pitted black olives, chopped

Cook the cauliflower in boiling, salted water until tender, 12 to 15 minutes. Drain and break it into florets. Place the florets and stems in a bowl and sprinkle with salt, pepper, and garlic. Add the celery. In a covered jar, shake the oil and vinegar to combine and pour the dressing over the salad; toss lightly. Garnish with the capers, anchovies, and olives.

Serves 4.

Squid Salad

1½ pounds squid
1 cup chopped celery
2 cloves garlic, minced
1 tablespoon chopped fresh
parsley
1 tablespoon lemon juice
3 tablespoons olive oil
1 tablespoon vinegar
1 teaspoon salt
¼ teaspoon freshly ground
black pepper
1 tablespoon freshly grated
Romano cheese

Remove and discard the tentacles, ink sac, and skin from the squid. Wash thoroughly. Cook the squid in 2 quarts of boiling water until it is tender, about 10 to 12 minutes; drain. Cut it into ½-inch-thick rings. Place the squid in a salad bowl. Add the celery, garlic, parsley, lemon juice, oil, vinegar, salt, and pepper. Mix well. Sprinkle the Romano cheese over the salad.

Serves 4.

Fish

Codfish Balls

1 pound codfish
4 medium potatoes, quartered
6 tablespoons milk
2 tablespoons butter
½ teaspoon salt
¼ teaspoon freshly ground
   black pepper
2 cloves garlic, minced
1 tablespoon minced parsley
¼ cup grated Parmesan cheese
⅛ teaspoon fennel seed
3 eggs
   Oil for frying
   Tomato Sauce (see page 79)

Cut the codfish into chunks and place them in a saucepan. Add the potatoes. Cover with water, bring it to a boil, and simmer until the potatoes are cooked, about 15 to 20 minutes. Drain. Mash the codfish and potatoes together. Mix in the milk, butter, and remaining ingredients, except the oil and Tomato Sauce. Form the mixture into balls of whatever size you like. Deep fry until golden brown. Serve with hot Tomato Sauce.

Serves 4 to 6.

When you're cooking a whole fish, make sure you wash the inside of it thoroughly. Any membrane left will add a bad flavor to your fish. Wash the cavity with salt and then rinse it with cold water.

Baked Trout with Mushrooms

4 small, whole trout
1½ cups all-purpose flour
½ cup vegetable oil
6 tablespoons butter
2 cups sliced mushrooms
1 tablespoon lemon juice
1 onion, finely chopped
1 cup bread crumbs
½ cup freshly grated Romano
   cheese
½ teaspoon salt
½ teaspoon freshly ground
   black pepper

Gut and wash the trout inside and out with salt water. Roll the trout in the flour and shake off any excess. Heat the oil and 2 tablespoons of the butter in a large frying pan and sauté the trout until golden on both sides, about 5 minutes each side. Remove the trout to a warm platter.

Preheat the oven to 350 degrees.

In a clean sauté pan, heat 2 tablespoons of the remaining butter; add the mushrooms and lemon juice. Cook, stirring, until the mushrooms are soft and give off their liquid. Transfer the mushrooms to an ungreased baking pan. Add the remaining 2 tablespoons of butter to the sauté pan, and sauté the onion until it is transparent.

Arrange the trout over the mushrooms in the baking pan and top with the onion. Combine the bread crumbs, cheese, salt, and pepper; sprinkle the mixture over the onions. Bake for 15 minutes.

Serves 4.

Trout Almandine

6 trout fillets
1 ½ cups bread crumbs
¼ cup freshly grated Romano
    cheese
1 teaspoon salt
¼ teaspoon freshly ground
    black pepper
¼ teaspoon dried oregano
6 cloves garlic, minced
8 tablespoons butter
¼ cup oil
    Juice of 1 lemon
½ cup sliced almonds

Wash the fillets with salted water. Dry them with paper towels. Mix together the bread crumbs, cheese, salt, pepper, oregano, and garlic. Dip each fillet into the bread crumb mixture, patting the crumbs on to make sure they adhere. Heat the butter and oil in a large skillet. Sauté the fillets on both sides until thoroughly cooked, about 5 minutes each side. Remove the fish to a warm platter. Add the lemon juice and almonds to the skillet; simmer and stir until the mixture is hot. Pour the sauce over the fillets and serve.

Serves 6.

Fried Smelts

2 pounds smelts, fresh or
    frozen
2 cups bread crumbs
¼ cup freshly grated Romano
    cheese
½ teaspoon salt
¼ teaspoon freshly ground
    black pepper
2 eggs, lightly beaten with 3
    tablespoons water
    Oil for frying
    Tomato Sauce (see page 79)

If the smelts are fresh, clean them by making an incision at the gills from head to tail, gut, and wash well. Dry with paper towels. Sprinkle with salt and pepper. Combine the bread crumbs, cheese, salt, and pepper, and mix thoroughly. Dip each smelt first into the eggs and then into the bread-crumb mixture. Fry in hot oil until golden brown, about 3 to 4 minutes on each side. Serve with hot Tomato Sauce.

Serves 4 to 6.

Broiled Salmon Steaks

4 large salmon steaks
8 tablespoons butter, melted
1 teaspoon salt
¼ teaspoon freshly ground
    black pepper
¼ teaspoon dried oregano
½ teaspoon minced garlic
    Sour Cream–Dill Sauce
    (recipe follows)

Preheat the broiler.

Brush the salmon steaks with the butter. Combine the salt, pepper, oregano, and garlic; rub into both sides of the steaks. Broil for 6 to 8 minutes on each side. Brush each steak with Sour Cream Dill Sauce, broil for 2 to 3 minutes more, and serve. Remaining sauce may be either poured over the steaks before serving or served on the side.

Serves 4 to 6.

Sour Cream–Dill Sauce

1 pint sour cream
1 small onion, minced
2 tablespoons dried dill weed
1 clove garlic, minced

Combine all the ingredients.

Salmon Loaf

2 cans salmon, or 2 pounds
    cooked fresh salmon
3 cups bread cubes, soaked in
    water and squeezed dry
1 cup freshly grated Romano
    cheese
1 teaspoon salt
¼ teaspoon freshly ground
    black pepper
¼ teaspoon dried oregano
½ teaspoon minced garlic
1 small onion, minced
5 eggs
2 tablespoons minced parsley
⅓ cup vegetable oil

Preheat the oven to 350 degrees.

Combine the salmon, bread, cheese, salt, pepper, oregano, garlic, onion, eggs, and parsley. Mix well. Oil your palms; shape the salmon mixture into a round or rectangular loaf. Place the loaf in a greased pan and bake until a knife inserted into the center of the loaf comes out clean, about 1 hour.

Serves 4.

Fried Squid

- 1 cup all-purpose flour
- 1 cup bread crumbs
- 1 teaspoon salt
- ¼ teaspoon freshly ground black pepper
- 1½ pounds squid, cleaned and cut crosswise into ½-inch-thick pieces
- Oil for frying

Combine the flour, bread crumbs, salt, and pepper. Roll the squid pieces in the mixture, coating well. Heat the oil in a large skillet. Fry the squid in the hot oil for 30 to 40 seconds, or until lightly browned.

Serves 4.

Stuffed Squid

- 1½ pounds squid, cleaned
- 2 cups bread crumbs
- ¾ cup freshly grated Romano cheese
- 2 eggs
- 1 teaspoon salt
- ¼ teaspoon freshly ground black pepper
- ½ teaspoon dried oregano
- 2 cloves garlic, minced
- 1½ cups Tomato Sauce (see page 79)
- ¼ cup white wine

Preheat the oven to 350 degrees.

Remove the tentacles, ink sac, and skin from the squid. Discard the ink sac and skin. Cut the tentacles into small pieces. In a small bowl, mix together the bread crumbs, ½ cup of the Romano cheese, the eggs, salt, pepper, oregano, garlic, and tentacle pieces. Fill the squid with the bread crumb mixture and place in a baking pan. Pour the Tomato Sauce over all. Sprinkle with the remaining Romano cheese. Pour the wine over all and bake for 1 hour.

Serves 4.

Tuna with Rice

- 1 cup cooked rice
- 1 7-ounce can tuna, drained and flaked
- 1 teaspoon salt
- ¼ teaspoon freshly ground black pepper
- ¼ teaspoon dried oregano
- 1 teaspoon minced garlic
- 4 tablespoons butter
- ¼ cup freshly grated Romano cheese

In a large saucepan, combine the rice, tuna, salt, pepper, oregano, and garlic. Cook over low heat. Stir in the butter and cheese until they melt.

Serves 4.

Italian Tuna Pie

6 eggs
½ cup milk
1 7-ounce can tuna, drained and flaked
½ cup freshly grated mozzarella cheese
½ cup freshly grated Romano cheese
1 teaspoon salt
¼ teaspoon dried oregano
¼ teaspoon freshly ground black pepper
½ teaspoon minced garlic
¼ teaspoon dried basil
1 9-inch unbaked pastry shell (see page 37)

Preheat the oven to 375 degrees.

Beat the eggs with the milk in a medium-size mixing bowl. Mix in the remaining ingredients except the pastry shell. Spoon the filling into the shell. Bake until a knife inserted in the center comes out clean, about 45 minutes.

Serves 4 to 6.

Casserole of Scallops

¼ cup vegetable oil
2 tablespoons butter
1½ pounds bay or sea scallops
1 medium onion, chopped
1 green pepper, chopped
1 cup sliced mushrooms
1 29-ounce can tomato sauce
1 teaspoon salt
¼ teaspoon freshly ground black pepper
¼ teaspoon dried oregano
½ cup white wine
½ teaspoon dried basil
3 cups cooked rice
½ cup freshly grated Romano cheese

Preheat the oven to 375 degrees.

Heat the oil and butter in a medium-size skillet. Sauté the scallops, turning frequently, for about 3 to 5 minutes. Remove the scallops with a slotted spoon and set aside. In the same skillet, add the onion, green pepper, and mushrooms. Cook the vegetables for a few minutes, stirring often. Add the remaining ingredients, except the rice, cheese, and scallops. Bring the mixture to a boil, reduce the heat, and cook for 10 to 15 minutes, stirring occasionally. Place the rice in a 4- or 5-quart casserole. Pour the sauce over the rice, add the scallops, and sprinkle on the cheese. Bake for 10 to 15 minutes.

Serves 4.

Scampi Italiano

8 tablespoons butter
2 cups sliced mushrooms
1 onion, chopped
2 cloves garlic, minced
1 teaspoon salt
2/3 teaspoon freshly ground
   black pepper
   Juice of 1 lemon
1/2 cup sweet vermouth
1 pound medium shrimp,
   cooked, peeled and deveined
1 cup bread crumbs, seasoned
   with a pinch of salt and
   freshly ground black pepper
3 tablespoons minced parsley
   Garlic Bread (see page 132)

Heat the butter in a skillet. Add the mushrooms, onion, garlic, salt, and pepper. Sauté for 5 minutes and then add the lemon juice. Cook for 2 to 3 minutes more. Add the vermouth. Place the shrimp evenly in the pan and sauté for 3 minutes on each side. Cover the shrimp with the seasoned bread crumbs. Stir, then sprinkle with parsley. Serve with Garlic Bread.

Serves 4.

Cioppino

1/4 cup olive oil
1/2 cup chopped green pepper
1/2 cup chopped onion
2 cloves garlic, minced
1/4 teaspoon dried oregano
1 29-ounce can tomato sauce
1 cup water
1/2 cup dry white wine
1 pound shrimp, peeled and
   deveined
2 tablespoons chopped fresh
   parsley
1 bay leaf
2 lobster tails, boiled, shelled,
   and cut into pieces
1 pound haddock fillets, cut
   into 2-inch pieces

Heat the oil in a large skillet. Add the green pepper, onion, garlic, and oregano. Sauté until the onions are transparent. Add the remaining ingredients, except the lobster and haddock. Simmer over low heat for 10 minutes. Add the lobster and haddock and cook for 10 minutes more, stirring occasionally.

Serves 4 to 6.

Fried Shrimp with Garlic Sauce

．．．．．．．．．．．．．．．．．．．．

         2 pounds shrimp
         1 teaspoon salt
         ½ teaspoon freshly ground
            black pepper
         ⅛ teaspoon dried oregano
         1 clove garlic, minced
         ¼ cup freshly grated
            Parmesan cheese
      1 ½ cups bread crumbs
         2 eggs
         ¼ cup milk
            Oil for frying
            Garlic Sauce (recipe
            follows)

Cook the shrimp in boiling, salted water until just pink. Peel and devein the shrimp; rinse in cold water and drain on paper towels. Mix together the salt, pepper, oregano, garlic, cheese, and bread crumbs. In another bowl, beat the eggs and milk together. Dip the shrimp in the egg mixture, then in the bread-crumb mixture. Heat the oil in a deep skillet and fry the shrimp until golden brown, about 3 minutes on each side. Pour the Garlic Sauce over the shrimp. Serve immediately.

Serves 4.

Garlic Sauce

      ¼ cup oil
      2 cloves garlic, minced
      1 teaspoon salt
      ¼ teaspoon dried oregano
      ¼ teaspoon freshly ground
         black pepper
      2 tablespoons chopped fresh
         parsley

Heat the oil in a skillet. Cook the garlic, salt, oregano, pepper, and parsley very slowly until the garlic browns lightly.

When I was in Palermo, Sicily, I first saw a fresh tuna. A friend of mine bought a 6- or 7-pound chunk of it, and it looked just like a big beef roast. She made slits in the tuna and stuffed the slits with garlic, oregano, parsley and basil leaves. Then she seasoned the tuna with salt and pepper and slowly browned it on all sides in oil. She put it in a big pot with the oil in which she browned it and simmered the tuna for 2 to 3 hours and served it with spaghetti. It was fabulous.

Chicken

Chicken Stew

1 tablespoon vegetable oil
8 tablespoons butter
4 stalks celery, chopped
2 teaspoons chopped fresh parsley
½ pound mushrooms, sliced
2 cloves garlic, minced
2 small onions, chopped
2 carrots, chopped
1 medium chicken, cut into pieces
1 6-ounce can tomato paste
6 ounces water (using the tomato paste can as a measure)
1 teaspoon salt
¼ teaspoon freshly ground black pepper
¼ teaspoon dried oregano
½ teaspoon minced garlic

Heat the oil and butter in a Dutch oven. Add the celery, parsley, mushrooms, garlic, onions, and carrots. Sauté until the onions are transparent. Add the chicken and brown on all sides. Add the tomato paste and water. Season with salt, pepper, oregano, and garlic. Cover and simmer over low heat until the chicken is tender, about 45 minutes. If the stew is too thick, add more water.

Serves 4.

Gene's Chicken Cordon Bleu

2 whole chicken breasts, skinned, boned, and halved
1½ teaspoons salt
½ teaspoon freshly ground black pepper
1 teaspoon minced garlic
¼ teaspoon dried oregano
2 slices Swiss cheese, halved
2 slices ham, halved
2 tablespoons minced parsley
2 cups corn flakes
½ teaspoon salt
¼ teaspoon freshly ground black pepper
½ cup freshly grated Romano cheese
2 eggs, beaten
2 cups cooked rice

Preheat the oven to 350 degrees.

Place each chicken breast half between 2 sheets of wax paper and pound until flat. Season the breasts with 1½ teaspoons salt, ½ teaspoon pepper, the garlic, and oregano. Lay ½ slice Swiss cheese and ½ slice ham on each chicken breast and sprinkle with parsley. Roll each up and secure with a toothpick if necessary.

Season the cornflakes with the remaining salt and pepper and the cheese. Dip each breast roll in the eggs and then roll in the corn flakes. Place the rolls on a greased baking sheet and bake for 25 to 30 minutes. Serve hot over rice.

Serves 4.

Chicken Parmesan

2 cups bread crumbs
½ cup freshly grated Parmesan
   cheese
1 teaspoon salt
¼ teaspoon freshly ground
   black pepper
2 cloves garlic, minced
¼ teaspoon dried oregano
1 2½- to 3-pound chicken, cut
   in pieces
2 eggs, lightly beaten
⅔ cup vegetable oil

Preheat the oven to 350 degrees.
   Combine the bread crumbs, cheese, salt, pepper, garlic, and oregano. Dip the chicken in the eggs and then in the bread-crumb mixture. Heat the oil in a large frying pan and fry the pieces on both sides just until the skin is browned. Remove them from the pan and place on a greased baking sheet. Bake for 1 hour.

Serves 4.

Macaroni and Chicken Pie

3 tablespoons butter
4 tablespoons oil
2 slices prosciutto, finely
   chopped
2 medium carrots, coarsely
   grated
2 small onions, finely
   chopped
1 small stalk celery, finely
   chopped
2½ cups cooked, cubed chicken
4 ounces mushrooms, sliced
1 teaspoon salt
1 teaspoon freshly ground
   black pepper
¼ teaspoon dried oregano
1 teaspoon minced garlic
1½ cups Chicken Broth (see
   page 40)
½ pound elbow macaroni,
   cooked and rinsed in cold
   water
¼ cup freshly grated
   Parmesan cheese
   Pie Crust (recipe follows)
1 egg, beaten with 1
   tablespoon water

Melt the butter and the oil in a 3-quart pot. Add the prosciutto, carrots, onions, and celery. Cook, stirring occasionally, until the onions are transparent. Add the chicken and mushrooms. Stir well and season with the salt, pepper, oregano, and garlic. Add the broth. Bring to a boil, lower the heat, and simmer, uncovered, for 30 minutes. Stir in the pasta and cheese.

Preheat the oven to 375 degrees.

Prepare the pie crust. Roll one pastry circle around the rolling pin and unroll into a 9-inch pie pan. Cut the dough evenly ½ inch from the edge of the pan. Pour the filling into the pie shell and cover with the top crust. Fold the edges under and flute. Cut slits here and there and brush with the egg mixture.

Bake until the crust is golden and the filling is bubbling, about 30 to 35 minutes.

Serves 6.

Pie Crust

2¼ cups all-purpose flour
  1 teaspoon salt
⅔ cup lard
¼ teaspoon vinegar
  4 tablespoons cold water

Combine the flour and salt in a mixing bowl. Cut in the lard until the dough resembles coarse meal. Mix in the vinegar and then the water, 1 tablespoon at a time, until the dough almost cleans the side of the bowl. Form into two balls. On a lightly floured board, roll out each ball to form a circle 2 inches larger than an inverted 9-inch pie pan.

Makes 1 double-crust 9-inch pie or 2 9-inch shells.

Baked Chicken Romano

1 3½- to 4-pound chicken, cut into pieces
½ cup vegetable oil
1 teaspoon salt
½ teaspoon freshly ground black pepper
1 teaspoon dried oregano
1 teaspoon minced garlic
1 cup sliced mushrooms
1 small onion, minced
¼ cup freshly grated Romano cheese

Preheat the oven to 375 degrees.

Place the chicken pieces in a shallow baking dish. Combine the oil, salt, pepper, oregano, and garlic and coat the chicken well with the mixture. Turn the chicken skin side up and bake for 30 minutes. Turn the chicken pieces and baste. Surround the chicken with the mushroom slices and onion, sprinkle with Romano cheese, and bake for 20 minutes more.

Serves 4.

Personally, I like Romano better than Parmesan cheese. It has a little more taste and body to it—it's a little sharper. When you add Romano cheese to something, you know it's there.

Chicken with Potatoes and Rosemary

1 3-pound chicken, cut into pieces
3 cloves garlic, minced
1 teaspoon salt
½ teaspoon freshly ground black pepper
2 tablespoons dried rosemary
2 bay leaves
1 cup dry white wine
¼ cup vegetable oil
4 potatoes, peeled and quartered

Preheat the oven to 350 degrees.

Put the chicken pieces in a bowl with the garlic, salt, pepper, rosemary, and bay leaves. Pour the wine and oil over the pieces and mix well. Place the chicken, skin side up, in a large casserole; pour the remaining mixture over the chicken. Place the potatoes around the chicken. Bake for 35 to 40 minutes, or until chicken is done.

Serves 4.

Chicken Balls

3 whole chicken breasts, skinned and boned
3 eggs
1 ½ teaspoons minced parsley
1 teaspoon dried basil
1 teaspoon salt
¼ teaspoon freshly ground black pepper
¼ teaspoon dried oregano
2 teaspoons minced garlic
1 ½ cups bread crumbs
4 tablespoons freshly grated Romano cheese

Preheat the oven to 375 degrees.

Finely grind the chicken and combine it with the remaining ingredients. When well mixed, make balls the size of golf balls. Place them on a greased cookie sheet and bake for 30 to 35 minutes.

Serves 6.

NOTE: These are also good in chicken soup. Drop the raw balls in simmering chicken soup and cook for 30 to 40 minutes.

Chicken with Spaghetti

8 tablespoons butter, melted
½ cup parsley leaves
2 cloves garlic, halved
   Salt and freshly ground black pepper, to taste
1 teaspoon dried basil
¼ teaspoon dried oregano
2 tablespoons vegetable oil
1 tablespoon lemon juice
1 2½- to 3-pound chicken, cut into pieces
½ pound spaghetti
   Parsley sprigs for garnish

Place the butter, parsley, garlic, salt, pepper, basil, and oregano in a food processor or blender. Cover; blend at high speed until the parsley is finely chopped. Set aside 3 tablespoons of the herb mixture for the chicken. Use the remainder to toss with the spaghetti.

Beat together the oil and lemon juice with a fork. Put the chicken on a broiler pan and brush each piece with the mixture. Sprinkle them with salt and pepper. Broil the chicken about 8 inches from the heating element until golden, about 20 minutes on each side. Brush each side with the reserved herb mixture during the last 4 minutes of broiling. About 15 minutes before the chicken is done, prepare the spaghetti and drain. Toss it with the herb mixture and place it on a platter. Arrange the chicken around the edge of the platter. Garnish with parsley sprigs.

Serves 4 to 6.

Chicken Vesuvio

1 2½- to 3-pound chicken, cut into pieces
4 potatoes, peeled and chopped
¼ cup vegetable oil
2 cloves garlic, minced
1½ teaspoons salt
¼ teaspoon freshly ground black pepper
¼ teaspoon dried oregano
½ cup dry sherry
1 cup Chicken Broth (see page 40)

Preheat the oven to 375 degrees.

Toss the chicken and potatoes with the oil, garlic, salt, pepper, and oregano. Place the chicken, skin side up, and the potatoes in a baking dish and bake until the chicken is tender, about 1 hour. Remove the baking dish from the oven and place the chicken in a large frying pan. Add the sherry and broth. Simmer for 5 minutes.

Serves 4.

Chicken Cacciatore

¼ cup olive oil
1 teaspoon salt
⅛ teaspoon freshly ground
 black pepper
1 2½- to 3-pound chicken, cut
 into pieces
1 clove garlic, minced
2 medium onions, chopped
12 mushrooms, sliced
1 green pepper, cut into large
 cubes
½ cup sliced black olives
1 cup Tomato Sauce (see page
 79)
½ cup dry white or red wine
1 cup hot Chicken Broth (recipe
 follows)
1 teaspoon dried basil
½ teaspoon dried mint
½ teaspoon dried oregano
1 bay leaf
1 pound pasta, cooked and
 drained
 Freshly grated Romano
 cheese

Preheat the oven to 350 degrees.

Heat the oil in a large skillet. Sprinkle the salt and pepper over the chicken and brown the pieces on both sides. Remove the chicken from the skillet. Add the garlic and onions and sauté until browned. Place the mushrooms, green pepper, and olives in a large baking dish. Arrange the chicken on top of the vegetables. Combine the tomato sauce, wine, broth, basil, mint, oregano and bay leaf and pour over the chicken. Bake until the chicken is tender, about 1 hour.

Serve the chicken over hot pasta and sprinkle with Romano cheese.

Serves 4.

Chicken Broth

 Chicken neck and giblets
1 quart water
2 tablespoons minced parsley
1 teaspoon salt
½ cup chopped onion
1 stalk celery, sliced

Place the chicken parts in a 2-quart saucepan and add the water. Bring it to a boil; reduce heat and skim off the grease. Add the parsley, salt, onion, and celery. Cook over low heat for 90 minutes.

Roast Stuffed Chicken

....

1 3- to 3½-pound chicken
  Salt, freshly ground black
  pepper, and dried oregano,
  to taste
4 cloves garlic, minced
¼ cup oil
2 small onions, chopped
2 stalks celery, chopped
¾ pound ground pork
1 teaspoon fennel seed
1 teaspoon salt
4 slices bread, soaked in water
  and squeezed dry
2 eggs, beaten
½ cup freshly grated Parmesan
  cheese
  Oil or butter

Preheat the oven to 375 degrees.

Rub the chicken with salt inside and out. Rinse under cold water. Season the cavity with salt, pepper, oregano, and half the garlic.

Heat the oil in a large skillet and brown the onions, celery, and remaining garlic. With a slotted spoon, remove the mixture to a bowl, leaving the oil in the skillet. Mix together the pork, fennel seed, and salt. Add the pork mixture to the skillet; cook until brown. Add pork mixture to the bowl with the onion mixture. Stir in the bread, eggs, and cheese. Mix together well and season to taste.

Fill the chicken cavity with the stuffing. Sew the skin closed over the cavity or use skewers to hold the stuffing in place; truss the chicken. Rub the oil or butter all over the chicken and place it in a roasting pan; roast for 1 hour.

Serves 4 to 6.

Meat

Stuffed Peppers

8 medium green peppers
1 pound ground beef
2 cloves garlic, minced
3 tablespoons chopped fresh
   parsley
4 slices bread, moistened in
   water and squeezed dry
2 eggs
   Salt and freshly ground black
   pepper, to taste
   Tomato Sauce, optional (see
   page 79)

Preheat the oven to 300 degrees.

Clean the peppers for stuffing by cutting off the tops and removing the seeds. Place the ground beef, garlic, parsley, bread, eggs, salt, and pepper in a bowl and mix well. Stuff the peppers with the meat mixture. Place the peppers in a greased roasting pan and bake for 30 to 40 minutes. Tomato Sauce may be spooned over the peppers, if desired.

Serves 8.

The worst thing that ever happened to American cooks was the invention of the measuring cup. You become so conscious of a fourth of this and an eighth of that. Learn to measure with your hands and your eyes when you're cooking. Learn what goes well together and don't be afraid to put in something if you like. Just taste, taste, taste.

Spadini

½ cup bread crumbs
¼ cup freshly grated Romano
   cheese
1 teaspoon minced parsley
¾ teaspoon salt
¼ teaspoon freshly ground
   black pepper
¼ teaspoon dried oregano
½ teaspoon minced garlic
4 slices rib-eye steak, ¼-inch
   thick
⅛ cup vegetable oil
2 slices ham, cut in half
2 slices Swiss cheese, cut in
   half
1 cup Tomato Sauce (see page
   79)
½ cup freshly grated mozzarella
   cheese

Mix together the bread crumbs, Romano cheese, parsley, salt, pepper, oregano, and garlic. Dip each steak in oil, then coat one side in the bread-crumb mixture. Lay the steaks flat, coated side down. Place ½ slice ham and ½ slice cheese on each steak. Top each with a spoonful of the bread crumbs and then a spoonful of Tomato Sauce. Roll up each steak like a jelly roll. Place the rolls on a baking dish and broil until each side is browned, about 4 minutes each side. Remove and put a spoonful of Tomato Sauce and 1 tablespoon mozzarella cheese on each piece. Broil until the cheese is melted.

Serves 4.

Baked Stuffed Zucchini

     2 medium zucchini
     1 medium onion, chopped
     1 clove garlic, minced
    ½ cup freshly grated Romano
        cheese
     1 pound ground beef
     1 cup cooked rice
     2 slices bread, soaked in water
        and squeezed dry
     2 eggs, lightly beaten
     1 teaspoon salt
    ½ teaspoon freshly ground
        black pepper
    ¼ teaspoon dried oregano
     4 slices mozzarella cheese

Preheat the oven to 350 degrees.

Cut the zucchini in half lengthwise and remove the pulp, leaving the shells ¼-inch thick. Chop the flesh. In a bowl, combine the onion, garlic, cheese, meat, rice, bread, eggs, salt, pepper, oregano, and chopped zucchini. Mix well. Stuff each zucchini half with the mixture. Place the halves in a greased baking dish and cover. Bake for 40 minutes. Place a slice of mozzarella cheese on each half and bake, uncovered, for 10 minutes more. Serve hot.

Serves 4.

Paesano Pie

    ½ cup Tomato Sauce (see
        page 79)
     1 pound ground beef
     2 eggs
    ½ cup bread crumbs
     1 small onion, finely chopped
     1 small green pepper, seeded
        and finely chopped
     2 cloves garlic, minced
     1 teaspoon salt
    ¼ teaspoon freshly ground
        black pepper
    ¼ teaspoon dried oregano
        Paesano Filling (recipe
        follows)
    ½ cup freshly shredded
        mozzarella cheese

Preheat the oven to 375 degrees.

In a large bowl, combine all the ingredients except the Paesano Filling and the cheese; mix well. Pat the mixture into a greased 10-inch pie plate, covering the bottom and sides evenly. Prepare the filling and pour it into the pie plate. Sprinkle with the mozzarella and cover the pie tightly with aluminum foil. Bake for 35 minutes. Remove the foil and continue baking for 15 minutes more. Serve hot.

Serves 4 to 6.

Paesano Filling

- ½ pound orzo or other small pasta, cooked, rinsed and drained
- 2 cups Tomato Sauce (see page 79)
- ½ teaspoon salt
- ¼ teaspoon freshly ground black pepper
- ¼ teaspoon dried oregano
- 1 teaspoon minced garlic
- ½ cup freshly grated Romano cheese

Combine all the ingredients in a bowl and stir well.

Meatball Puffs

- 1 pound ground beef
- 1 medium onion, minced
- 3 slices bread, soaked in water and squeezed dry
- 2 eggs
- 1 teaspoon salt
- ¼ teaspoon freshly ground black pepper
- ¼ teaspoon dried oregano
- 1 teaspoon minced garlic
- ½ cup freshly grated Parmesan cheese
- 1 teaspoon fennel seeds
- 2 tablespoons all-purpose flour
- 1 cup milk
  Tomato Sauce (see page 79)

Mix all the ingredients except the Tomato Sauce in a bowl and refrigerate for 1 hour.

Preheat the oven to 350 degrees.

Place the mixture in muffin cups and bake for 30 minutes. Serve the puffs with hot Tomato Sauce.

Serves 4.

Italian Rump Roast

- 1 4-pound rump roast
- 4 cloves garlic, slivered
- 1½ teaspoons salt
- ½ teaspoon freshly ground black pepper
- 1 teaspoon dried oregano
- 1 teaspoon dried basil
- ½ cup olive oil
- 1 large onion, sliced
- ¼ cup chopped fresh parsley
- 1½ cups dry red wine

Preheat the oven to 375 degrees.

Cut slits in the meat and insert the garlic slivers. Combine the salt, pepper, oregano, and basil on a plate. Brush the roast with the oil and then roll in the salt mixture. Heat the remaining oil in a large, ovenproof skillet. Sauté the onion and parsley until the onion is transparent. Add the roast and brown it on all sides. Pour the wine over the meat, place the skillet in the oven, and bake for about 1 hour, basting from time to time. Use a meat thermometer to ensure thorough cooking.

Serves 8.

Tiella

1 cup water
4 medium potatoes, peeled and sliced
4 medium zucchini, sliced
2 small green peppers, diced
2 small onions, chopped
1 pound ground beef
1½ cups Tomato Sauce (see page 79)
¼ cup vegetable oil
1 teaspoon salt
½ teaspoon freshly ground black pepper
¼ teaspoon dried oregano
1 teaspoon minced garlic
1 cup freshly grated Romano cheese

Preheat the oven to 325 degrees.

Grease an 8-by-10-inch baking pan. Pour the water into the pan. Alternately layer the potatoes, zucchini, peppers, onions, and ground beef. Repeat the layers until all the vegetables and meat have been used. First pour the Tomato Sauce and then drizzle the oil over the layers. Season with the salt, pepper, oregano, and garlic. Sprinkle the cheese over the top and bake until the vegetables are tender, about 1 hour.

Serves 4.

Liver alla Veneziana

½ cup vegetable oil
2 medium onions, chopped
2 cloves garlic, minced
1 tablespoon chopped fresh parsley
1 pound calf's liver, cut into strips
½ cup all-purpose flour
1 teaspoon salt
¼ teaspoon freshly ground black pepper
½ cup dry white wine

Heat the oil in a large saucepan. Add the onions, garlic, and parsley, and sauté until the onions are transparent. Remove the onions, garlic, and parsley from the pan and set aside. Dredge the liver in the flour. Sauté the liver until slightly browned. Add the reserved onion mixture, salt, and pepper. Pour the wine over all and simmer over low heat for 15 minutes.

Serves 4.

Beef and Cabbage Casserole

¼ cup vegetable oil
2 medium onions, chopped
2 cloves garlic, minced
1½ pounds ground beef
¼ cup freshly grated Romano cheese
1 teaspoon salt
¼ teaspoon freshly ground black pepper
2 medium heads cabbage, cut into large pieces
1½ cups Tomato Sauce (see page 79)
¼ cup shredded mozzarella cheese

Preheat the oven to 350 degrees.

Heat the oil in a large skillet. Add the onions and garlic and sauté until the onions are transparent. Add the beef, Romano cheese, salt, and pepper. Sauté until the meat is lightly browned. Using a 3-quart casserole, alternately layer the cabbage and the meat mixture until all is used. Pour the Tomato Sauce over all. Sprinkle with the mozzarella cheese and bake, uncovered, for 90 minutes.

Serves 4.

Don't season your food at the table. Then it's too late. It has to be done in your kitchen. Food has so much more flavor if the seasonings are cooked right into it.

Beef and Zucchini Casserole

2 tablespoons vegetable oil
1 pound ground beef
3 cups bread crumbs
½ cup freshly grated Romano cheese
1 teaspoon salt
½ teaspoon freshly ground black pepper
¼ teaspoon dried oregano
1 teaspoon minced garlic
6 small zucchini, peeled and sliced
2 medium onions, chopped
3 green peppers, julienned
4 potatoes, peeled and sliced
½ cup vegetable oil

Preheat the oven to 375 degrees.

Heat the oil in a large skillet; brown the beef lightly. Mix in the bread crumbs, cheese, salt, pepper, oregano, and garlic. In a greased 8-by-10-inch baking dish, alternately layer the zucchini, onions, green peppers, and potatoes. Sprinkle the meat mixture over each layer. Repeat the layers until all ingredients are used, ending with potatoes. Sprinkle the oil over the top layer. Bake, covered, until the potatoes are tender, about 1 hour.

Serves 4.

Italian Ground Beef Casserole

2 tablespoons butter
2 tablespoons vegetable oil
1 large onion, diced
2 cloves garlic, minced
1 green pepper, diced
1 pound ground beef
½ cup Tomato Sauce (see page 79)
3 medium potatoes, peeled and diced
1 teaspoon salt
¼ teaspoon freshly ground black pepper
¼ teaspoon dried oregano
2 cups cooked rice,
6 thin slices ham
½ cup water

Preheat the oven to 375 degrees.

Heat the butter and oil in a large saucepan. Add the onion, garlic, green pepper, and ground beef. Sauté until the onion is transparent. Add the Tomato Sauce, potatoes, salt, pepper, and oregano, and cook over low heat for 15 minutes. Place the rice in a 3-quart casserole. Lay the ham over the rice. Spoon the ground meat mixture over the ham. Add the water. Bake for 30 minutes.

Serves 4 to 6.

Pepper Steak

¼ cup vegetable oil
1 pound sirloin steak, cut into strips 5 inches long
4 green peppers, julienned
3 cloves garlic, minced
2 medium onions, chopped
1 cup sliced mushrooms
1 teaspoon salt
¼ teaspoon freshly ground black pepper
1 cup chopped tomatoes
1 cup dry white wine
2 cups cooked rice, or 1 pound flat noodles, cooked and drained
½ cup freshly grated Romano cheese

Heat the oil in a large saucepan. Add the steak, green peppers, garlic, onions, and mushrooms. Sauté until the onions are transparent. Stir in the salt and pepper. Add the tomatoes and wine. Reduce the heat and cook, stirring occasionally, until the meat is browned, about 30 minutes. Serve over a bed of rice or flat noodles. Sprinkle with Romano cheese before serving.

Serves 4.

Braciole

2 tablespoons chopped fresh parsley
1 clove garlic, minced
½ cup bread crumbs
1 tablespoon freshly grated Parmesan cheese
1 small onion, finely chopped
2 hard-boiled eggs, peeled and diced
2 strips bacon, diced
1 teaspoon salt
Freshly ground black pepper, to taste
Pinch of dried oregano
1½ pounds round steak, pounded on both sides
1 egg, beaten
2 tablespoons all-purpose flour
¼ cup vegetable oil
¾ cup water
1½ cups Tomato Sauce (see page 79)

Preheat the oven to 350 degrees.

Place the parsley, garlic, bread crumbs, cheese, onion, hard-boiled eggs, bacon, salt, pepper, and oregano in a bowl and mix thoroughly. Lay the steak flat on a work surface. Spread the bread-crumb mixture on top of the steak. Fold in the edges of the steak and roll it up. Tie it securely with string.

Dip the rolled and tied steak in the beaten egg, then in the flour. Heat the oil in a skillet; sauté the steak on all sides until golden brown. Place it in a roasting pan. Add the water, pour the Tomato Sauce over all, and roast for 45 minutes. Cut the meat into 1½-inch-thick slices and serve.

Serves 4 to 6.

Sicilian Steak

1½ cups bread crumbs
¼ cup freshly grated Romano cheese
1 teaspoon salt
½ teaspoon freshly ground black pepper
½ teaspoon oregano
1 teaspoon minced garlic
4 sirloin steaks, 6 to 8 ounces each, flattened and cut into strips ½-inch wide
Vegetable oil
2 green peppers, julienned
1½ cups sliced mushrooms
½ cup white wine

Combine the bread crumbs, cheese, and half the salt, pepper, oregano, and garlic. Dip the meat in oil and then into the bread-crumb mixture. Heat ¼ cup oil in a large skillet and sauté the steak on both sides until browned. Remove the steak from the skillet and set aside. Add the peppers and mushrooms and sauté until soft. Add the steak to the peppers and mushrooms and stir gently. Season with the remaining salt, pepper, oregano, and garlic. Pour the wine over all and simmer over low heat for 5 minutes.

Serves 4.

Costolette

2 cups bread crumbs
1½ cups freshly grated Romano cheese
1 teaspoon salt
¼ teaspoon freshly ground black pepper
2 cloves garlic, minced
2 teaspoons minced parsley
¼ teaspoon dried basil
6 veal chops, thinly sliced
2 eggs, lightly beaten
½ cup vegetable oil

Mix together the bread crumbs, cheese, salt, pepper, garlic, parsley, and basil. Dip the chops into the egg, then into the bread-crumb mixture. Heat the oil in a large skillet and sauté the chops on both sides until golden brown.

Serves 6.

You can make bread crumbs that are much better than the ones you buy in the supermarket. Dry stale bread in the oven. Grate it and keep it in a covered jar in the refrigerator. It lasts forever. If you wish, you can season it to taste.

Braciole of Veal

2 cups bread crumbs
½ cup freshly grated Romano cheese
2 tablespoons minced parsley
1 teaspoon salt
¼ teaspoon freshly ground black pepper
½ teaspoon minced garlic
1½ pounds veal, sliced into 6 pieces
¼ cup vegetable oil
6 slices ham
6 slices Swiss cheese
¾ cup Tomato Sauce (see page 79)
Freshly grated mozzarella cheese

Preheat the oven to 375 degrees.
Combine the bread crumbs, Romano cheese, parsley, salt, pepper, and garlic. Dip the veal in the oil, then coat both sides in the bread-crumb mixture. Place a slice of ham and a slice of Swiss cheese on each piece of veal. Sprinkle a little of the bread-crumb mixture on top and roll up each slice of veal securing each with string or a toothpick. Place the rolls on a greased baking sheet and bake for 20 minutes.
Before removing the braciole from the oven, place a tablespoon of Tomato Sauce and a sprinkling of mozzarella cheese on each roll. Continue baking until the cheese melts.

Serves 6.

Veal al Caruso

4 thin slices veal
2 cups bread crumbs
¼ cup freshly grated Romano cheese
2 teaspoons minced parsley
1 teaspoon salt
¼ teaspoon freshly ground black pepper
½ teaspoon minced garlic
¼ cup vegetable oil
4 slices eggplant, sautéed until browned on both sides
1 cup Bolognese sauce (see page 77)
4 slices mozzarella cheese

Preheat the broiler.

With a mallet flatten the veal between 2 sheets of wax paper so that it is paper thin. Mix the bread crumbs, cheese, parsley, salt, pepper, and garlic. Dip the veal into the oil then into the bread-crumb mixture, and coat on both sides. Heat the remaining oil in a frying pan and sauté the veal until it is browned on both sides. Place the veal on the broiler pan and top with 1 slice of the eggplant, some sauce, and a slice of cheese. Broil the veal until the cheese is melted.

Serves 4.

Braised Veal Shanks

5 tablespoons butter
1 onion, chopped
2 carrots, chopped
2 stalks celery, chopped
2 cloves garlic, minced
8 veal shanks
All-purpose flour
Salt and freshly ground black pepper
½ cup oil
1 cup dry white wine
1 teaspoon basil
1 cup beef broth or 1 cup Chicken Broth (see page 40)
1 29-ounce can tomato purée
1 tablespoon minced parsley
2 bay leaves

Preheat the oven to 375 degrees.

Melt the butter in a Dutch oven or roasting pan. Add the onion, carrots, celery, and garlic. Sauté for 10 minutes; remove from the heat. Rub the veal shanks with the flour and season with salt and pepper. Heat the oil in a skillet and cook the shanks until golden brown on both sides; place them over the vegetables in the Dutch oven or roasting pan. Pour off the oil from the skillet; add the wine to the skillet and heat until it boils briskly. Stir in the basil, broth, tomato purée, parsley, and bay leaves. Bring the wine mixture to a boil and pour it over the veal shanks. If the liquid doesn't cover the bottom half of the veal shanks, add more broth. Bake, covered, until the shanks are tender, about 1½ hours. Season with salt and pepper to taste.

Serves 8.

Saltimbocca

¼ cup vegetable oil
1 tablespoon butter
8 thin slices veal (cut from the leg or shoulder), pounded
Pinch of salt
½ teaspoon freshly ground black pepper
Dried sage, to taste
1 clove garlic, minced
8 slices prosciutto
¼ cup freshly grated mozzarella cheese
½ cup white wine
½ pound small mushrooms, halved

Heat the oil and butter in a skillet. Brown the veal lightly on both sides. Remove the veal from the pan. Season the veal with the salt, pepper, sage, and garlic. Put a slice of prosciutto on each slice of veal. Sprinkle with mozzarella cheese. Roll up the veal slices and filling and fasten with toothpicks. Return the rolls to the skillet and add the wine and mushrooms. Simmer slowly over low heat until most of the liquid has evaporated. Serve immediately.

Serves 4.

Veal Roast with Carrots and Potatoes

1 3-pound veal shoulder or rump roast
¼ pound bacon, diced
Pinch of salt
½ teaspoon freshly ground black pepper
2 cloves garlic, minced
3 tablespoons minced parsley
¼ cup oil
3 medium onions, quartered
6 carrots, quartered
4 to 6 medium potatoes, peeled and quartered
1 cup water

Preheat the oven to 350 degrees.

Cut slits in the veal with a sharp knife. Put a piece of bacon in each slit. Mix the salt, pepper, garlic, and parsley together. Put a little of the mixture into each slit. Heat the oil in a roasting pan and brown the veal on all sides. Remove the roasting pan from the heat. Arrange the vegetables around the browned veal, add the water, cover, and roast for 1½ hours. A meat thermometer can be used to ensure thorough cooking.

Serves 6.

Veal Parmesan

1½ pounds veal (cut from the leg or shoulder), sliced ¼-inch thick
1 cup bread crumbs
½ cup freshly grated Parmesan cheese
1 clove garlic, minced
½ teaspoon salt
⅛ teaspoon freshly ground black pepper
½ cup vegetable oil
2 eggs, beaten
⅓ to ¾ cup Tomato Sauce (see page 79)
½ cup freshly grated mozzarella cheese

Preheat the oven to 375 degrees.

Cut the veal into 3-by-3-inch pieces. Mix the bread crumbs, ¼ cup of the Parmesan cheese, the garlic, salt, and pepper. Heat the oil in a skillet. Dip the veal in the eggs, then in the bread-crumb mixture; fry until golden brown on both sides.

Arrange the veal on a lightly greased cookie sheet or baking dish. Spoon a little Tomato Sauce over each piece; sprinkle with the remaining Parmesan cheese and the mozzarella. Bake until the cheese is melted, about 15 minutes.

Serves 4.

Meat Loaf

1½ pounds ground beef
½ pound ground pork
1 teaspoon salt
¼ teaspoon freshly ground black pepper
2 cloves garlic, minced
3 eggs, lightly beaten
½ cup freshly grated Romano cheese
1 tablespoon chopped fresh parsley
4 thin slices ham
1 cup Tomato Sauce (see page 79)
4 slices mozzarella cheese

Preheat the oven to 375 degrees.

Combine the beef, pork, salt, pepper, garlic, eggs, Romano cheese, and parsley. Mix well. Place the meat mixture on wax paper and press to form a 1-inch-thick rectangle. Place the ham on top of the meat and roll it up from the long side. Place the meat in a greased 9-by-12-inch baking pan. Pour the Tomato Sauce over the top of the meat loaf. Lay the mozzarella cheese over the top of the loaf. Bake until the meat is done, about 1 hour. Cool for 10 minutes before slicing.

Serves 6.

Meat Loaf, Italian Style

¼ cup oil
1 pound ground beef
1 pound ground pork
1 clove garlic, minced
2 tablespoons finely chopped
  fresh parsley
4 eggs
4 slices bread, soaked in water
  and squeezed dry
¾ cup freshly grated Romano
  cheese
  Salt to taste
½ teaspoon freshly ground
  black pepper
4 hard-boiled eggs, peeled

Preheat the oven to 375 degrees.

In a bowl mix all the ingredients except the hard-boiled eggs. Grease a loaf pan. Shape half the meat into an oblong or oval shape in the pan. Arrange the hard-boiled eggs lengthwise down the center. Cover the eggs completely with the remaining meat. Smooth the meat with oiled hands; bake for 1 hour.

Serves 6.

Sweet-and-Sour Meatballs

1 pound ground beef
½ pound ground pork
3 eggs, lightly beaten
½ cup freshly grated Romano
  cheese
2 cloves garlic, minced
2 tablespoons chopped fresh
  parsley
1 teaspoon salt
½ teaspoon freshly ground
  black pepper
½ teaspoon fennel seeds
4 or 5 slices bread, soaked in
  water and squeezed dry
3 onions, chopped
1 6-ounce can tomato paste
1½ cups water
½ cup wine vinegar
2 tablespoons brown sugar
  Salt to taste
½ teaspoon freshly ground
  black pepper

Preheat the oven to 375 degrees.

Mix together the meats, eggs, cheese, garlic, parsley, 1 teaspoon salt, ½ teaspoon pepper, fennel seeds, and bread; shape into balls about 1 inch in diameter. Place the meatballs on a greased baking pan with low sides and bake until they are browned all over, about 20 minutes.

Put the pan drippings in a large saucepan. Sauté the onions in the drippings until they are transparent. Add the tomato paste, water, vinegar, sugar, salt, and ½ teaspoon pepper. Stir well. Add the meatballs and simmer slowly for 1 hour.

Serves 4 to 6.

Pork Chops alla Mama D

3 tablespoons vegetable oil
1 medium onion, chopped
2 green peppers, chopped
2 cloves garlic, minced
½ pound mushrooms, sliced
6 center-cut pork chops
½ teaspoon salt
¼ teaspoon freshly ground
   black pepper
1 bay leaf
½ teaspoon dried rosemary
½ cup dry white wine

Heat the oil in a large frying pan. Add the onion, peppers, garlic, and mushrooms; sauté until the onions are transparent. Add the chops and brown on both sides. Add the salt, pepper, bay leaf, and rosemary. Stir in the wine. Simmer, covered, over low heat until the chops are cooked, about 20 to 30 minutes.

Serves 6.

Porchetta

2 teaspoons salt
¼ teaspoon freshly ground
   black pepper
¼ teaspoon dried oregano
2 cloves garlic, minced
2 teaspoons dried sage
2 teaspoons dried basil
1 bay leaf, crushed
1½ teaspoons dried rosemary
1 4- to 5-pound boneless
   pork loin

Preheat the oven to 350 degrees.

Mix all the seasonings except one teaspoon of the salt. Spread the spices on the inner side of the pork loin. Roll the meat and tie securely with string. Place the pork in a roasting pan. Add enough water to come halfway up the sides of the meat. Season the top of the meat with the remaining 1 teaspoon of salt. Bake until the meat is thoroughly cooked, about 2 hours. A meat thermometer can be used to ensure thorough cooking.

Serves 4 to 6.

Minestra

¼ cup vegetable oil
2 pounds pork or beef, cut into 1-inch pieces
2 medium onions, chopped
1 teaspoon salt
¼ teaspoon freshly ground black pepper
½ teaspoon minced garlic
3 small tomatoes, cut into small pieces
5 carrots, peeled and cut into small pieces
4 potatoes, peeled and cut into small pieces
1 pound green beans, cut into small pieces
1 cup water

Heat the oil in a large skillet. Add the meat and brown lightly. Add the onions, salt, pepper, garlic, tomatoes, carrots, potatoes, and green beans. Stir in the water and cook over low heat until the meat and vegetables are tender, about 1 hour.

Serves 4.

Piemontese Pork

4 tablespoons butter
2 tablespoons olive oil
1½ pounds pork tenderloin, thinly sliced and pounded flat
¾ cup white wine
1 teaspoon salt
½ teaspoon dried oregano
½ teaspoon dried basil
2 tablespoons minced parsley
   Freshly ground black pepper to taste
   Sliced provolone cheese

Preheat the oven to 400 degrees.
   Heat the butter and oil in a large skillet. Add the pork slices and brown each well on both sides. Stir in the wine, salt, oregano, basil, parsley, and pepper. Simmer all over low heat for 15 minutes, basting the meat frequently. Place the pork in a shallow baking dish. Pour the sauce from the pan over the pork. Place a slice of provolone cheese on each slice of pork. Bake until the cheese melts, about 10 minutes.

Serves 3 to 4.

Pork Chops Neapolitan Style

         2 cloves garlic, minced
       1/4 cup vegetable oil
         4 pork chops, rib or loin
         2 green peppers, chopped
         1 teaspoon salt
       1/4 teaspoon freshly ground
            black pepper
            Pinch of dried oregano
         2 fresh ripe tomatoes,
            chopped, or 1/2 cup crushed
            Italian tomatoes
         3 tablespoons wine vinegar
       1/4 pound mushrooms, sliced

Brown the garlic in the oil in a skillet. Add the pork chops and brown on both sides. Add the green peppers, salt, pepper, oregano, tomatoes, wine vinegar, and mushrooms. Cook, covered, over low heat for about 45 minutes; add a little water as needed.

Serves 4.

Roast Loin of Pork with Potatoes

         1 3- to 4-pound pork loin roast
       1/4 cup oil
            Salt to taste
       1/2 teaspoon freshly ground
            black pepper
       1/4 teaspoon dried thyme
         2 cloves garlic, minced
         3 sprigs parsley, chopped
         2 cups water
         6 potatoes, peeled and halved

Preheat the oven to 350 degrees.

Rub the pork with the oil and season with the salt, pepper, thyme, garlic and parsley; place in a roasting pan. Roast the meat until done, about 2 1/2 hours. One hour before the meat is done, add the water and potatoes to the pan; baste often. Use a meat thermometer to ensure thorough cooking.

Serves 6 to 8.

> I cook like your grandmothers did when they came to this country. No fancy utensils. Cook with what you have. Cooking for your family with love is the most important thing.

Polenta with Sausage

3 tablespoons oil
1 pound hot or mild Italian sausages, sliced
2 small onions, sliced
1 pound fresh mushrooms, sliced
Salt
¼ teaspoon freshly ground black pepper
⅛ teaspoon dried oregano
2 cloves garlic, minced
1 29-ounce can crushed tomatoes
4 cups water
1½ cups cornmeal
¼ cup freshly grated Romano cheese

Heat the oil in a skillet. Sauté the sausages and onions until the sausages are lightly browned. Add the mushrooms, a pinch of salt, the pepper, oregano, and garlic. Sauté for 5 minutes more. Add the tomatoes; simmer slowly for 1 hour. Bring the water and a pinch of salt to a boil in a saucepan. Stir in the cornmeal and continue boiling until the mixture thickens. (Keep stirring the mixture so it doesn't stick and burn.) Cover, lower the heat, and cook the mixture slowly, stirring frequently, for 5 to 10 minutes. (Total cooking time should be 20 to 30 minutes.) Transfer the cornmeal to a warm platter; spread the sausage-mushroom mixture on it. Sprinkle with cheese and serve.

Serves 4.

Eggplant with Sausage

½ cup vegetable oil
1 large (or 2 medium) eggplant, sliced
1½ cups bread crumbs
½ cup freshly grated Romano cheese
2 teaspoons salt
¼ teaspoon freshly ground black pepper
2 tablespoons chopped fresh parsley
2 cloves garlic, minced
1 pound ground pork
2 small onions, minced
2 teaspoons crushed fennel seeds
3 hard-boiled eggs, peeled and sliced
1½ cups Tomato Sauce (see page 79)
½ cup cubed mozzarella cheese

Preheat the oven to 350 degrees.

Heat the oil in a large skillet. Brown the eggplant on both sides. Remove the slices from the pan and set aside.

In a small bowl, mix the bread crumbs, Romano cheese, 1 teaspoon of the salt, the pepper, parsley, and garlic. In a separate bowl, combine the pork, onions, remaining salt, and fennel; mix well. Place the pork mixture in the skillet and sauté until crumbly.

Grease an 8-by-10-inch baking pan. Alternately layer the eggplant, meat mixture, a few slices of hard-boiled egg, and the bread-crumb mixture until all ingredients are used.

Spread the Tomato Sauce over the top. Place the mozzarella cheese over the sauce. Cover the baking pan with aluminum foil and bake for 1 hour.

Serves 4 to 6.

Macaroni and Sausage Pie

- ½ pound sweet Italian sausages
- 1 recipe Pie Crust (see page 37)
- 1½ cups elbow macaroni, cooked and rinsed in cold water
- 8 eggs, beaten
- ½ cup freshly grated Romano cheese
- 1 teaspoon salt
- ¼ teaspoon freshly ground black pepper
- ¼ teaspoon dried oregano
- ½ teaspoon minced garlic
- 1 teaspoon chopped fresh parsley
- 1 egg yolk beaten with 1 tablespoon water

Preheat the oven to 375 degrees.

Put the sausages into a shallow baking pan and bake for 40 minutes, turning them halfway through the cooking time. Cut them into ¼-inch pieces. Lower the oven heat to 350 degrees.

Roll one of the pastry circles around the rolling pin and unroll it into a 9-inch pie pan. Cut the dough evenly ½ inch from the edge of the pan.

Combine the sausages and remaining ingredients except the egg mixture. Pour the combined ingredients into the pie pan and cover with the top crust. Fold the edges under and flute. Cut slits here and there in the top crust and brush it with the egg mixture. Bake for 1 hour. Serve hot.

Serves 6.

Italian Sausage and Cheese Fondue

1 pound hot or mild Italian sausage, removed from casing
1 small onion, minced
1½ tablespoons oil
1½ cups Tomato Sauce (see page 79)
1 tablespoon cornstarch
1 tablespoon minced garlic
1 teaspoon salt
½ teaspoon dried oregano
½ teaspoon fennel seeds
½ teaspoon freshly ground black pepper
¼ pound sharp cheddar cheese, grated
¼ pound mozzarella cheese, grated

In a fondue pot, brown the sausage and onion in the oil. Add the Tomato Sauce, cornstarch, garlic, salt, oregano, fennel seeds, and pepper. Mix well. Cook until the mixture is thick. Add the cheddar cheese and mozzarella a little at a time, and stir until the cheese is melted. Serve with Garlic Bread (see page 132).

Serves 6 to 8.

Baked Ham with Tomatoes and Cheese

2 1-inch-thick slices ham
2½ cups Italian plum tomatoes, drained and chopped
½ teaspoon salt
¼ teaspoon dried thyme
¼ cup freshly grated Parmesan cheese

Preheat the oven to 350 degrees.

Place the ham slices in a baking dish. Spoon the tomatoes over the slices and sprinkle them with the salt and thyme. Cover the baking dish with aluminum foil and bake until the ham is tender, about 45 minutes. Five minutes before the end of the baking time, uncover the dish and sprinkle on the Parmesan cheese. Bake until the cheese is melted.

Serves 4.

Some domestic cheeses are better than imports. Whenever you can, taste the cheese before you buy. I've tasted both domestic and imported provolone—and ended up buying the domestic, which costs less. If the cheese is prepackaged, you'll have to take a chance on it.

Breast of Lamb, Sicilian Style

1 2- to 2½-pound breast of
   lamb, trimmed of fat
   Salt and freshly ground
   black pepper to taste
1 cup bread crumbs
1 tablespoon minced scallions
1 tablespoon minced parsley
1 clove garlic, minced
½ teaspoon dried thyme

Preheat the oven to 450 degrees

   Place the lamb, meaty side down, in a large baking dish. Sprinkle with the salt and pepper. Bake for 30 minutes; reduce the heat to 375 degrees. Turn the lamb meaty side up and bake for 15 minutes. Combine the remaining ingredients and mix well. Sprinkle the bread-crumb mixture over the lamb and bake until the crumbs are nicely browned, about 15 to 20 minutes. Cut the lamb into serving pieces.

Serves 4.

Lamb Stew with Peas

¼ cup vegetable oil
2 tablespoons butter
1½ pounds lamb stew meat
2 medium onions, chopped
2 cloves garlic, minced
1¼ teaspoons salt
¼ teaspoon freshly ground
   black pepper
1 pound peas, fresh or frozen

Heat the oil and butter in a Dutch oven. Add the meat and brown lightly. Add the onions, garlic, salt, and pepper; simmer, stirring occasionally, until the meat is tender, about 20 to 30 minutes. Add the peas. Cook over low heat until the peas are tender, about 3 to 5 minutes.

Serves 4.

Pasta & Sauces

Meatless Lasagna

½ cup oil
½ cup chopped onions
3½ cups Tomato Sauce (see page 79)
1 tablespoon fresh basil leaves or 1 teaspoon dried basil
1 teaspoon salt
¼ teaspoon freshly ground black pepper
¼ teaspoon dried oregano
1 tablespoon minced garlic
1 pound lasagna noodles
Filling (recipe follows)
½ cup freshly grated Romano cheese
1 cup freshly grated mozzarella cheese

Heat the oil in a heavy saucepan. Add the onions and sauté until they are transparent. Add the Tomato Sauce, basil, salt, pepper, oregano, and garlic. Simmer slowly for 1½ hours.

Preheat the oven to 375 degrees.

While the sauce is simmering, cook the pasta according to package directions until al dente and make the filling. Cover the bottom of a 2-inch-deep rectangular lasagna pan with ½ cup of the sauce and completely cover that with a layer of noodles. Spread half of the filling over the noodles. Alternate the layers of noodles and filling, ending with noodles. Pour 1½ cups of the sauce over the top. Sprinkle with the Romano and mozzarella cheeses. Cover the pan with plastic wrap and then aluminum foil and bake until the mixture is heated through, about 1 hour. Before serving, cut the lasagna into squares. Heat the remaining sauce, spoon some over each square, and serve.

Serves 4 to 6.

Filling

2 pounds ricotta cheese
¾ cup freshly grated Romano cheese
4 eggs
1 teaspoon salt
¼ teaspoon freshly ground black pepper
3 sprigs parsley, chopped

Combine all ingredients.

Homemade noodles are very easy to make. Some people think making noodles is a big thing, but all you need is flour, a little water, a couple of eggs, and some salt. Knead the dough until it's stiff and roll it out like pie dough. Then cut the dough into thin strips. Some little old Italian ladies can make noodles so thin and precise that they look as though they were cut by a machine. My noodles aren't perfect—but at least they're homemade, and I know what I'm eating.

Meatless Spaghetti

¼ cup oil
1 green pepper, chopped
1 large onion, finely chopped
2 cloves garlic, minced
½ pound fresh mushrooms, sliced
1 teaspoon salt
¼ teaspoon freshly ground black pepper
3 cups Tomato Sauce (see page 79)
¼ cup red wine
1 pound spaghetti
½ cup freshly grated Romano cheese

Heat the oil in a saucepan. Add the green pepper, onion, garlic, mushrooms, salt, and pepper. Sauté until the onions are transparent. Add the Tomato Sauce and wine. Lower the heat; simmer for 2½ hours. Cook the spaghetti according to package directions until al dente; drain. Put the pasta on a platter, sprinkle it with cheese, pour the sauce over it, and serve.

Serves 4.

Shells with Mustard Greens

1 pound mustard greens, cleaned
¼ cup vegetable oil
2 cloves garlic, minced
1 teaspoon salt
¼ teaspoon freshly ground black pepper
1 pound shell macaroni, cooked al dente and drained

Bring to a boil in a 6-quart kettle enough water to cover the mustard greens. Add the mustard greens and cook for 5 to 7 minutes. Drain, reserving 1 cup of the cooking liquid. Heat the oil in a large saucepan. Add the garlic and sauté for 3 minutes. Add the mustard greens, reserved cooking liquid, salt, and pepper. Mix lightly. Stir in the cooked pasta and reduce heat. Simmer for 3 to 5 minutes.

Serves 4.

Sausage and Spaghetti Casserole

....

1 pound hot or sweet Italian
  sausage
¼ cup vegetable oil
1 medium onion, chopped
2 cloves garlic, minced
2 cups sliced mushrooms
3 cups Tomato Sauce (see
  page 79)
1 teaspoon salt
¼ teaspoon freshly ground
  black pepper
¼ teaspoon dried oregano
1 pound spaghetti, cooked al
  dente and drained
½ cup freshly grated Romano
  cheese
½ cup freshly grated mozzarella
  cheese

Preheat the oven to 350 degrees.

Bake the sausage for 45 minutes and remove it from oven. Raise the oven temperature to 375 degrees.

Cut the sausage into ½-inch pieces. Heat the oil in a large skillet and sauté the onion, garlic, mushrooms, and sausage for 5 minutes. Stir in the Tomato Sauce, salt, pepper, and oregano. Simmer for 1 hour. Place the spaghetti in a 4-quart casserole. Sprinkle the Romano cheese over the pasta, and pour the cooked tomato sauce on top. Sprinkle the mozzarella cheese over the sauce. Bake the casserole for 15 minutes, or until the cheese is golden.

Serves 4.

Spaghetti with Tuna

....

¼ cup vegetable oil
1 medium onion, chopped
3 cloves garlic, minced
1 teaspoon chopped fresh
  parsley
1 7-ounce can tuna, drained
  and flaked
10 pitted black olives, sliced
2 cups Tomato Sauce (see
  page 79)
1 teaspoon salt
¼ teaspoon freshly ground
  black pepper
¼ teaspoon dried oregano
1 pound spaghetti
  Freshly grated Parmesan
  cheese

Heat the oil in a large saucepan. Sauté the onion, garlic, and parsley for 3 minutes. Add the tuna, olives, and Tomato Sauce. Season with salt, pepper, and oregano. Simmer for 45 minutes. Cook the spaghetti according to package directions until al dente; drain. Spoon the tuna mixture over the spaghetti. Sprinkle the Parmesan cheese over all and serve.

Serves 4 to 6.

Pita Pizza

1 cup sliced, sautéed
   mushrooms
1 teaspoon salt
1/4 teaspoon freshly ground
   black pepper
1/8 teaspoon dried oregano
1 small onion, finely chopped
1/4 cup freshly grated Romano
   cheese
1/2 cup cubed mozzarella cheese
4 2-ounce pita breads
3 tablespoons Tomato Sauce
   (see page 79)
4 thin slices mozzarella cheese

Preheat the oven to 350 degrees.

Mix the mushrooms, salt, pepper, oregano, onion, and both cheeses in a bowl. Open the pita breads and spread one side of each with Tomato Sauce; fill with the mushroom-cheese mixture and close the pocket. Bake for 15 minutes, then brush each pita with the remaining sauce and place a slice of mozzarella on top of the sauce. Bake until the cheese is melted and serve.

Serves 4.

Calzone

Pizza Dough (recipe follows)
Filling (recipe follows)

Prepare the pizza dough.
   Preheat the oven to 375 degrees.
   Prepare the filling.
   Divide the dough into 4 pieces. Roll each piece into a circle 6 inches in diameter. Put 1/4 filling in the center of each, fold the dough in half, and seal the edge with a fork. Put the half moons on a greased baking sheet and bake them until the dough is golden brown, 20 to 25 minutes.

Makes 4 6-inch calzones.

Pizza Dough

2 1/4-ounce envelopes active dry
   yeast
2 cups warm water
2 eggs
1 teaspoon salt
4 to 5 cups all-purpose flour

Sprinkle the yeast over the warm water and set aside until the yeast is foamy. Add the eggs, salt, and flour. On a floured surface, knead the dough until a soft ball forms, adding more flour if necessary; continue kneading until soft and smooth. Place the dough in a bowl, cover it, and let it rise in a warm place until double in bulk.

Filling

- 1 pound ricotta cheese
- 1 teaspoon salt
- 2 eggs
- ½ cup freshly grated Romano cheese
- 1 egg
- ½ teaspoon freshly ground black pepper
- ¼ teaspoon dried oregano
- 1 teaspoon minced garlic
- 1 pound hot or mild Italian sausage, cooked and sliced ¼-inch thick

Mix all the ingredients together.

It's impossible to tell anyone exactly how long to cook pasta. Pasta varies from brand to brand—that which contains the most durum wheat or semolina takes the longest to cook. One pound of pasta will serve 4 to 6 people.

Pasta alla Bassa Italia

- ¼ cup vegetable oil
- 3 cloves garlic
- 1 medium onion, chopped
- 2 cups sliced mushrooms
- 1 green pepper, finely chopped
  Salt, to taste
  Freshly ground black pepper, to taste
- 3 cups peeled, crushed tomatoes, fresh or canned
- 1 pound spaghetti
- ½ cup freshly grated Romano cheese

Heat the oil in a saucepan and add the garlic, onion, mushrooms, and green pepper. Sauté until the onion is soft. Add the salt, pepper, and tomatoes; cook for 1½ hours. Cook the spaghetti according to package directions until al dente; drain. Combine the pasta with the sauce. Sprinkle cheese over all and serve.

Serves 4.

Italian Baked Spaghetti Casserole

....

    1 pound ground beef
    1 small onion, minced
  ½ cup chopped celery,
       including leaves
    2 cloves garlic, minced
3½ cups Tomato Sauce (see
       page 79)
    1 teaspoon salt
  ½ teaspoon freshly ground
       black pepper
    1 teaspoon fennel seeds
    1 pound spaghetti, cooked al
       dente and drained
  ¼ cup freshly grated Romano
       cheese

Preheat the oven to 375 degrees.

In a large skillet, cook the meat, onion, celery, and garlic, stirring, until the meat is brown and crumbly. Add the Tomato Sauce, salt, pepper, and fennel seeds. Cook, covered, for 30 minutes, stirring frequently. In a 1½-quart casserole alternately layer the sauce and spaghetti. Sprinkle the cheese over all and bake for 25 minutes.

Serves 4 to 6.

Doc's Fresh Tomato Spaghetti

....

    8 plum tomatoes, diced
  ½ cup vegetable oil
    3 cloves garlic, minced
    1 onion, minced
1½ teaspoon salt
  ½ teaspoon freshly ground
       black pepper
  ¼ teaspoon dried thyme
    1 pound spaghetti
  ½ cup freshly grated Romano
       cheese

Place the diced tomatoes in a bowl. Add the oil, garlic, onion, salt, pepper, and thyme. Cover the bowl and refrigerate for two days.

Cook spaghetti according to package directions until al dente; drain. Remove the tomatoes from the refrigerator, spoon them over the hot spaghetti, sprinkle the cheese over all, and serve.

Serves 4.

Pasta Primavera

1 pound spaghetti
2 cups sliced carrots
3 cups chopped broccoli
3 tablespoons butter
1 teaspoon salt
½ teaspoon freshly ground
   black pepper
½ cup parsley
1 onion, finely chopped
½ cup heavy cream
   Freshly grated Parmesan
   cheese

Cook the spaghetti according to package directions until al dente; drain. Meanwhile, steam the carrots and broccoli until just tender. Heat the butter in a large skillet. Add the salt, pepper, parsley, and onion; sauté until the onion is soft. Add the heavy cream, carrots, broccoli, and spaghetti. Cook for 1 or 2 minutes until the cream is heated, place all on a platter, sprinkle with cheese, and serve.

Serves 4 to 6

Sam's Spaghetti-Shrimp Dish

¼ cup vegetable oil
3 cloves garlic, minced
1 large onion, chopped
2 cups sliced mushrooms
1 cup minced green peppers
1 pound baby shrimp, peeled
   and deveined
1 teaspoon salt
¾ teaspoon freshly ground
   black pepper
1 pound spaghetti
1 cup Seasoned Bread Crumbs
   (recipe follows)

Heat the oil in a sauté pan; add the garlic and onion. Sauté until the onion is soft. Add the mushrooms and peppers, and sauté until the peppers are soft. Add the shrimp and cook for 5 minutes; season with the salt and pepper. Cook the spaghetti according to package directions until al dente; drain. Combine the pasta with the other ingredients. Cover all with Seasoned Bread Crumbs and serve.

Serves 4.

Seasoned Bread Crumbs

1 cup bread crumbs
¼ cup freshly grated Romano
   cheese
¼ teaspoon salt
¼ teaspoon dried oregano
¼ teaspoon freshly ground
   black pepper

Mix all ingredients together.

Sam's Tomato and Clam alla Linguine

½ pound butter
2 cloves garlic, chopped
1 onion, chopped
2 cups sliced mushrooms
1 teaspoon salt
1 teaspoon freshly ground black pepper
3 tomatoes, diced
1 cup chopped clams, with juice from can
1 pound linguine
¼ cup freshly grated Romano cheese

Heat the butter in a sauté pan. Add the garlic, onion, mushrooms, salt, and pepper. Sauté for 5 minutes; add the tomatoes and sauté until the tomatoes are soft and blended. Add the clams and their juice and sauté over low heat for 10 to 15 minutes. Cook the linguine according to package directions until al dente; drain. Mix the pasta with the tomato-clam sauce and place on a platter. Sprinkle the cheese over the linguine and serve.

Serves 4.

Spaghetti with Cod

¼ cup olive oil
Salt
½ teaspoon freshly ground black pepper
2 cloves garlic, minced
1½ pounds codfish
3 tablespoons chopped fresh parsley
3½ cups Tomato Sauce (see page 79)
2 stalks celery, finely chopped
1 cup peas
1 pound spaghetti
½ cup freshly grated Romano cheese

Heat the oil in a large skillet and add the salt, pepper, garlic, codfish, parsley, Tomato Sauce, and celery. Cook over low heat for 2 hours. Add the peas for the last 5 minutes.

Cook the spaghetti according to package directions until al dente; drain. Combine the pasta with the sauce and place on a platter. Sprinkle with cheese and serve.

Serves 4 to 6.

Chicken Liver Spaghetti Sauce

½ cup vegetable or olive oil
3 cloves garlic, minced
2 green peppers, sliced lengthwise
1 onion, minced
2 cups sliced mushrooms
1 teaspoon dried basil
1 teaspoon salt
½ teaspoon freshly ground black pepper
½ teaspoon dried oregano
1½ pounds chicken livers
3½ cups Tomato Sauce, (see page 79)
1 pound spaghetti
½ cup freshly grated Romano cheese

Heat the oil in a skillet. Add the garlic, peppers, and onion and sauté until the onion is transparent. Add the mushrooms, basil, salt, pepper, oregano, and chicken livers. Cook, stirring frequently, over low heat for 15 minutes. Add the Tomato Sauce and simmer for 40 minutes.

Cook the spaghetti according to package directions until al dente; drain. Mix the pasta with some of the chicken liver sauce on a platter. Pour the rest of the sauce over the pasta, sprinkle with the Romano cheese, and serve.

Serves 4.

Spaghetti with Raisins

1 pound spaghetti
½ cup olive or vegetable oil
1 small onion, chopped
4 cloves garlic, minced
½ cup finely chopped pignoli or walnuts
1½ teaspoons salt
1 teaspoon freshly ground black pepper
½ cup raisins
5 tablespoons butter
½ cup freshly grated Romano cheese

While the spaghetti is cooking according to package directions, heat the oil in a skillet. Add the onion, garlic, nuts, salt, and pepper. Cook, stirring, for about 5 minutes. Add the raisins and cook 5 minutes longer. Toss the drained spaghetti with the sauce; add the butter and mix well until it is melted. Put the pasta on a platter and sprinkle the Romano cheese over all.

Serves 4 to 6.

Pasta e Pesto

1 pound spaghetti
3 cups basil leaves
½ cup parsley
⅔ cup olive oil
4 cloves garlic
½ cup freshly grated Romano
   cheese
1 teaspoon salt
¼ teaspoon freshly ground
   black pepper
½ cup pignoli or walnuts
   Freshly grated Romano
   cheese

While the spaghetti is cooking according to package directions, purée the remaining ingredients in a blender or food processor to make a paste. Mix ½ cup of the pasta water with the paste to make a sauce; toss the sauce with the spaghetti. Sprinkle more grated cheese over all.

Serves 4.

Mama D's Pesto Sauce

1 large bunch parsley with
   stems, chopped
1 cup fresh basil leaves
2 tablespoons butter, melted
½ cup olive oil
4 cloves garlic
½ cup freshly grated Romano
   cheese
1 teaspoon salt
¼ teaspoon freshly ground
   black pepper
¼ teaspoon dried oregano
½ cup pignoli

Place the ingredients in a blender or food processor and purée to a smooth paste. Scrape the sauce into a screw-top jar. Cover the sauce with a film of olive oil and store, covered, in the refrigerator.

Makes about 3 cups.

There is a difference of night and day between fresh and dried herbs. You never know how long prepared herbs have been in the jars. So use the fresh herbs whenever you can.

Bolognese Sauce

 1 pound boneless beef chuck or round
 ½ pound boneless veal shoulder
 ½ pound boneless fresh pork butt
 2 tablespoons butter
 2 tablespoons olive oil
 2 small onions, chopped
 2 cloves garlic, minced
 2 stalks celery, chopped
 2 28-ounce cans plum tomatoes
 ¼ pound mushrooms, sliced
 1 cup dry white wine
 2 tablespoons chopped fresh parsley
 2 teaspoons dried basil, crushed
 ¼ teaspoon freshly ground nutmeg
 1 teaspoon salt
 ¼ teaspoon freshly ground black pepper
 ¼ teaspoon dried oregano

Cut the beef, veal, and pork into ¾-inch cubes. Melt the butter with the oil in a 4-quart casserole over medium-high heat. Add the meat and sauté, turning the cubes so they brown evenly.

Reduce the heat to medium and add the onions, garlic, and celery. Cook, stirring occasionally, until the onions are transparent. Add the tomatoes, crushing them in your hand as you add them, and the liquid from the cans. Stir in the remaining ingredients. Raise the heat and bring the sauce to a boil. Lower the heat and simmer, uncovered, for 2½ hours. Stir occasionally to avoid burning.

Makes about 8 cups.

Bolognese Tomato Sauce

 ¼ cup oil
 1 onion, diced
 ¼ pound salt pork, diced
 ½ pound hot or mild sausage, sliced
 ½ pound beef, cubed
   Salt to taste
 2 cloves garlic, minced
 1 teaspoon dried basil
 ¼ teaspoon freshly ground black pepper
 1 tablespoon minced parsley
 1 bay leaf
 1 29-ounce can crushed tomatoes
 1 6-ounce can tomato paste
 6 ounces water (using the tomato paste can as a measure)
 ½ cup dry white wine
 ¼ pound mushrooms, sliced

Heat the oil in a saucepan. Add the onion and salt pork and sauté until the onion is golden brown. Add the sausage and beef and brown slowly. Add the salt, garlic, basil, pepper, parsley, bay leaf, tomatoes, tomato paste, and water. Stir well. Add the wine and mushrooms. Cook slowly for 2 hours.

Serves 4 to 6.

Fresh Mushroom Sauce

3 tablespoons olive oil
1 pound mushrooms, sliced
2 medium onions, finely chopped
3 cloves garlic, minced
1 28-ounce can plum tomatoes
1 teaspoon salt
¼ teaspoon freshly ground black pepper
1 tablespoon chopped parsley
3 or 4 fresh basil leaves, or ¼ teaspoon dried basil
1 6-ounce can tomato paste
6 ounces water (using the tomato paste can as a measure)

Heat the oil in a heavy 10- to 12-inch skillet over medium heat. Add the mushrooms, onions, and garlic; sauté until the onions are transparent. Add the tomatoes, crushing them in your hand as you add them, and the liquid from the can. Raise the heat, stir in the remaining ingredients, and bring to a boil. Lower the heat and simmer, uncovered, for 1½ to 2 hours. Stir occasionally to avoid burning.

Makes about 4 cups.

Marinara Sauce

3 tablespoons olive oil
2 small onions, finely chopped
2 cloves garlic, minced
2 large carrots, finely chopped
2 large stalks celery, finely chopped
1 28-ounce can plum tomatoes
1 teaspoon salt
¼ teaspoon freshly ground black pepper

Heat the oil in a heavy 10- to 12-inch skillet over medium heat. Add the onions, garlic, carrots, and celery; sauté until the onions are transparent. Add the tomatoes, crushing them in your hand as you add them, and the liquid from the can. Raise the heat and add the salt and pepper, stirring to blend. Bring to a boil. Reduce the heat and simmer, uncovered, for 1½ to 2 hours. Stir occasionally to avoid burning.

Makes about 4 cups.

Mama D's Favorite Pasta Sauce

. . . .

    2 tablespoons olive oil
    2 pounds pork spareribs, cut
       into pieces
    1 medium onion, finely
       chopped
    2 cloves garlic, minced
    1 28-ounce can plum
       tomatoes
    1 6-ounce can tomato paste
    6 ounces water (using the
       tomato paste can as a
       measure)
    1 teaspoon salt
    ½ teaspoon freshly ground
       black pepper
    1 teaspoon minced garlic
 1 ½ teaspoons fennel seeds

Heat the oil in a 5-quart casserole over medium-high heat; brown the spareribs. Add the
onion and 2 cloves minced garlic and sauté
until the onion is transparent. Add the
tomatoes, crushing them in your hand as you
add them, and the liquid from the can. Add
the tomato paste and the water. Raise the heat
and add the remaining ingredients. Bring to a
boil, stirring to mix. Reduce the heat and simmer, uncovered, until the meat starts to fall
away from the bone, about 2 hours. Stir often
to keep the sauce from sticking to the bottom
of the pan.

Serves 4 to 6.

Tomato Sauce

. . . .

    ½ cup oil
    1 medium onion, finely
       chopped
    2 cloves garlic, minced
    1 28-ounce can plum tomatoes
    1 6-ounce can tomato paste
    6 ounces water (using the
       tomato paste can as a
       measure)
    2 tablespoons chopped parsley
    1 teaspoon dried basil
    1 teaspoon salt
    ¼ teaspoon freshly ground
       black pepper
    ¼ teaspoon dried thyme

Heat the oil in a heavy 10- to 12-inch skillet
over medium heat. Add the onion and garlic;
sauté until the onion is transparent. Add the
tomatoes, crushing them in your hand as you
add them, and the liquid from the can. Add
the remaining ingredients and stir to mix.
Raise the heat and bring the sauce to a boil.
Lower the heat and simmer, uncovered, for
1 ½ to 2 hours. Stir occasionally to avoid
burning.

Makes about 4 cups.

Fresh Tomato Sauce

2 pounds very ripe plum
　tomatoes
½ cup olive oil
2 medium onions, finely
　chopped
3 cloves garlic, minced
1 teaspoon salt
¼ teaspoon freshly ground
　black pepper
¼ teaspoon dried oregano
1 tablespoon crushed, dried
　basil leaves, or 6 to 8 fresh
　basil leaves
1 tablespoon chopped fresh
　parsley

Plunge the tomatoes into boiling water for 12
seconds. Peel the tomatoes and chop them
coarsely. Heat the oil in a heavy 10- to 12-inch
skillet over medium heat. Add the onions and
garlic; sauté until the onions are transparent.
Add the tomatoes, salt, pepper, oregano,
basil, and parsley.

　Cook, uncovered, over low heat for 2
hours. Stir occasionally to avoid burning.

Makes about 4 cups.

NOTE: I belong to the old school and cook
my sauces for a long time, but not as long as
my mother did. She cooked them all day. To
my mind, a tomato sauce needs to be cooked
for 2 hours or more to develop a mellow flavor
and lose all the tartness of the tomatoes. I can
afford to do this because cooking is my busi-
ness and the kitchen is my office. For those of
you who can't spend the time, I point to my
son. He makes delicious sauces that cook for
only 30 minutes. Taste your sauce after that
period of time and if you like it, serve it. Rules
are made to be broken, even my own. How-
ever, if the sauce still tastes tart to you, try
adding a pinch of baking soda or a teaspoon
or so of sugar.

Spaghetti with Mama D's White Clam Sauce

4 tablespoons oil
1 large onion, chopped
2 cloves garlic, minced
1 cup minced clams
1 cup bottled clam juice
1 tablespoon chopped parsley
½ teaspoon freshly ground
　black pepper
1 pound spaghetti
¼ cup freshly grated Romano
　cheese

Heat the oil in a heavy 8-inch skillet over medium heat. Add the onion and garlic; sauté
until the onion is transparent. Add the clams,
clam juice, parsley and pepper. Bring to a boil.
Reduce the heat and simmer, uncovered, for
about 30 minutes.

　While the sauce is simmering, cook the
pasta according to package directions until al
dente. Drain and place on a warmed platter.
Sprinkle with the cheese. Top with the clam
sauce and serve immediately.

Serves 4 to 6.

NOTE: I know cheese isn't supposed to be
served with clam sauce, but my customers love
it. If you want to follow the rules, leave it out.

Baked Ziti with Mushrooms and Sausage

··

    1 pound sweet or hot Italian
      sausage
    1 pound ziti
    ½ pound mushrooms, sliced
    ½ cup freshly grated Romano
      cheese
    1 teaspoon salt
    1 teaspoon freshly ground
      black pepper
    ¼ teaspoon dried oregano
    ½ teaspoon minced garlic
    2 cups Tomato Sauce (see
      page 79)
      Topping (recipe follows)
    ½ cup freshly shredded
      mozzarella cheese

Preheat the oven to 375 degrees.

Place the sausage in a shallow baking pan and bake until the sausage is browned and cooked through, about 40 minutes. Leave the oven at 375 degrees. Cut the sausage into ¼-inch pieces. Prepare the topping.

Cook the pasta according to package directions until just al dente. Drain and place in a mixing bowl. Add the sliced sausage, mushrooms, Romano cheese, salt, pepper, oregano, and garlic to the bowl. Mix with 1 cup of the Tomato Sauce. Transfer the mixture to the baking pan and pour the remaining sauce on top. Sprinkle with the bread-crumb Topping.

Bake, uncovered, for 45 minutes. Sprinkle the mozzarella over all and return the pan to the oven for 10 minutes or until the cheese is melted.

Serves 4 to 6.

Topping

    1 cup bread crumbs
    ½ cup freshly grated Romano
      cheese
    ½ teaspoon salt
    ¼ teaspoon freshly ground
      black pepper
    ¼ teaspoon dried oregano
    ½ teaspoon minced garlic
    2 teaspoons chopped fresh
      parsley

Combine all ingredients and mix well.

Spaghettini with Cod and Black Olive Sauce

4 tablespoons olive oil
2 onions, finely chopped
2 cloves garlic, minced
1½ pounds cod fillets, cut into pieces
1 28-ounce can plum tomatoes
1 pound pitted black olives
1 teaspoon salt
¼ teaspoon freshly ground black pepper
⅛ teaspoon dried oregano
1 bay leaf
1 pound spaghettini
½ cup freshly grated Romano cheese

Heat the oil in a heavy 10- to 12-inch skillet over medium heat. Add the onions and garlic; sauté until the onions are transparent. Add the cod and cook, stirring, for 3 to 5 minutes.

Add the tomatoes, crushing them in your hand as you add them, and the liquid from the can. Stir in the remaining ingredients except the pasta and cheese. Bring to a boil. Lower the heat and simmer, uncovered, for about 2 hours.

Cook the pasta according to package directions until al dente. Drain and place on a warmed platter. Spoon the sauce over the pasta, sprinkle with the cheese, and serve.

Serves 4 to 6.

Spaghetti and Tuna Casserole

1 pound spaghetti
3 hard-boiled eggs, peeled and sliced
1 7-ounce can tuna, drained and flaked
1 pound peas
½ cup freshly grated Romano cheese
1 teaspoon salt
¼ teaspoon freshly ground black pepper
1¼ cups milk
2 tablespoons butter

Preheat the oven to 375 degrees.

Break the pasta into small pieces and cook according to package directions just until al dente; drain. Put ⅓ of the pasta into a greased 3-quart casserole. Cover with ½ of the eggs, tuna, and peas, and sprinkle with 2 tablespoons of the cheese. Repeat. Cover with the remaining pasta and sprinkle with the remaining cheese. Add the salt and pepper to the milk and heat. Pour the milk over the pasta and dot with the butter. Bake, uncovered, for 15 to 20 minutes.

Serves 4 to 6.

Mama D's Spaghetti with Ricotta

1 pound spaghetti
1 cup ricotta cheese
¼ cup freshly grated Parmesan cheese
1 egg, beaten
½ teaspoon salt
¼ teaspoon freshly ground black pepper
⅛ teaspoon dried oregano
½ teaspoon garlic powder
4 tablespoons butter
¼ cup freshly shredded mozzarella cheese

Cook the pasta according to package directions until al dente.

While the pasta is cooking, combine the ricotta cheese with the Parmesan, egg, salt, pepper, oregano, and garlic powder. Taste for seasoning.

When the pasta is done, drain, leaving a little water in the pot. Add the butter to the pot and return the pasta to it, tossing well. Stir in the ricotta cheese mixture and transfer all to a baking dish. Top with the shredded mozzarella and put under the broiler until the mozzarella is melted but not browned.

Serves 4 to 6.

Perciatelli with Eggplant and Green Olive Sauce

4 tablespoons olive oil
2 cloves garlic, minced
2½ cups Tomato Sauce (see page 79)
1 teaspoon salt
¼ teaspoon freshly ground black pepper
¼ teaspoon dried oregano
2 tablespoons chopped fresh basil leaves
½ cup chopped, pitted green olives
1 small (about 1 pound) eggplant, peeled and diced
1 pound perciatelli
½ cup freshly grated Romano cheese

Heat the oil in a heavy 8-inch skillet over medium heat. Add the garlic and sauté until the garlic is golden. Add the Tomato Sauce, seasonings, and olives. Bring the mixture to a boil, lower the heat, and simmer, uncovered, for 20 minutes. Add the eggplant and simmer until the eggplant is tender, about 15 minutes.

While the eggplant is simmering, cook the pasta according to package directions until al dente; drain. Place the pasta on a warmed platter and pour the sauce over it; mix gently. Sprinkle with cheese and serve hot.

Serves 4 to 6.

Rotelle and Italian Meatballs

4 cups Tomato Sauce (see page 79)
Italian Meatballs (recipe follows)
1 pound rotelle
½ cup freshly grated Romano cheese

Prepare the sauce and the meatballs. Before serving, add the meatballs to the sauce and cook until the meatballs are warmed through.

Cook the pasta according to package directions until al dente; drain. Put the pasta on a warmed platter and mix with about 2 cups of the sauce. Sprinkle with the cheese and place the meatballs on top. Serve with the remaining sauce and additional grated cheese.

Serves 4 to 6.

Italian Meatballs

½ pound ground beef
¼ pound ground veal
¼ pound ground pork
4 slices stale bread, soaked in water, squeezed dry, and torn into pieces
3 eggs
½ cup freshly grated Romano cheese
2 tablespoons chopped fresh parsley
2 cloves garlic, minced
1½ teaspoons salt
¼ teaspoon freshly ground black pepper
⅛ teaspoon dried oregano
½ teaspoon fennel seed

Preheat the oven to 375 degrees.

Place the meats in a large bowl and add the bread. Add the remaining ingredients and mix well, but gently, with your hands. Oil your hands and form the mixture into 12 balls. Put the meatballs on a shallow baking pan and bake until the meatballs are browned and cooked through, about 25 to 30 minutes.

NOTE: This recipe makes about 10 to 12 large balls, 30 medium balls, or 50 small balls. Bake the medium balls for about 18 minutes and the small balls for about 12 minutes.

Baked Noodles, Italian Style

4 cups Tomato Sauce (see
   page 79)
1 pound fettuccine, cooked,
   rinsed in cold water, and
   drained
2 cups freshly shredded
   mozzarella cheese
1/2 cup freshly grated Romano
   cheese

Preheat the oven to 375 degrees.

Spread about 1/2 cup of the Tomato Sauce in the bottom of a 13 1/2-by-9-by-2-inch baking dish. Cover with 1/3 of the pasta and sprinkle with 1/2 cup mozzarella. Repeat the layers. Put the remaining pasta on top and cover with the rest of the sauce. Sprinkle the remaining mozzarella and then the Romano on top. Cover the baking dish tightly with aluminum foil and bake for 25 to 30 minutes. Serve hot.

Serves 4 to 6.

Mostaccioli with Potatoes and Basil

4 tablespoons oil
4 medium potatoes, peeled and
   diced
2 small onions, finely chopped
2 cloves garlic, minced
2 cups Tomato Sauce (see
   page 79)
1 teaspoon salt
1/4 teaspoon freshly ground
   black pepper
2 tablespoons chopped fresh
   basil leaves or 2 teaspoons
   dried basil
2 tablespoons chopped fresh
   parsley
1 pound mostaccioli or rigatoni
1/2 cup freshly grated Romano
   cheese

Heat the oil in a heavy 8-inch skillet. Add the potatoes, onions, and garlic; sauté until the onions are transparent. Add the Tomato Sauce and the salt, pepper, basil, and parsley. Cook, covered, over low heat until the potatoes are tender, about 20 minutes.

Cook the pasta according to package directions until al dente; drain. Put the pasta into a warmed deep bowl. Stir in the potato mixture. Serve with grated cheese on the side.

Serves 4 to 6.

Mostaccioli with Braciole

1 pound round steak, about ½-inch thick
2 hard-boiled eggs, peeled and chopped
3 slices bacon, chopped
½ cup bread crumbs
¼ cup freshly grated Romano cheese
1 teaspoon salt
½ teaspoon freshly ground black pepper
4 tablespoons olive oil
2 small onions, minced
1 clove garlic, minced
1 29-ounce can tomato purée
1 pound mostaccioli
½ cup freshly grated Romano cheese

Preheat the oven to 375 degrees.

Score the steak lightly on both sides and spread it out on a flat surface. Mix the eggs, bacon, bread crumbs, ¼ cup grated Romano cheese, salt, and pepper in a bowl. Spread the mixture over the steak. Roll up the steak, and tie it with string.

Heat the oil in a casserole large enough to hold the braciole. Add the onions and garlic. Cook over medium-high heat, stirring, until the onions are transparent. Add the braciole and brown on all sides. Pour the tomato purée over the steak and bring it to a boil. Cover the casserole and bake for 2 hours.

Cook the pasta according to the package directions until al dente; drain. Put the pasta on a warmed platter.

Remove the braciole from the casserole and pour the sauce from it over the pasta.
Sprinkle with the ½ cup grated Romano. Cut the braciole into 1-inch-thick slices. Arrange the slices on top of the pasta and sauce. Serve hot.

Serves 4 to 6.

Baked Maruzzine with Cauliflower

1 pound maruzzine, fusilli, or rigatoni, cooked, rinsed in cold water, and drained
1 small head cauliflower, separated into florets, cooked, and drained
4 tablespoons butter, melted
½ cup freshly grated Romano cheese
1 teaspoon salt
¼ teaspoon freshly ground black pepper
¼ teaspoon dried oregano
½ teaspoon minced garlic
½ cup freshly shredded mozzarella cheese

Preheat the oven to 375 degrees.

Combine the cooked pasta and cauliflower in a shallow baking dish. Pour the melted butter on top and sprinkle with the grated Romano, salt, pepper, oregano, and garlic. Toss to mix and then sprinkle with the shredded mozzarella. Bake the dish until the mozzarella is melted, about 10 minutes.

Serves 4 to 6.

Mafalda with Tuna Sauce

- 4 tablespoons oil
- 2 cloves garlic, minced
- 1 28-ounce can plum tomatoes
- ½ teaspoon salt
- ¼ teaspoon freshly ground black pepper
- ⅛ teaspoon dried oregano
- 1 2-ounce can anchovy fillets, drained
- 1 tablespoon capers, chopped
- 1 7-ounce can tuna, drained and flaked
- 1 pound mafalda or rotoni

Heat the oil in a heavy 10- to 12-inch skillet over medium heat. Add the garlic and sauté until the garlic is golden. Add the tomatoes, crushing them in your hand as you add them, and the liquid from the can. Add the remaining ingredients except the pasta. Bring to a boil, lower the heat, and simmer, uncovered, until the sauce is slightly thickened, about 2½ hours. Stir occasionally to prevent burning.

When the sauce is almost ready, cook the pasta according to package directions until al dente; drain. Put the pasta into a warmed deep bowl. Add half the sauce and mix gently. Serve with the remaining sauce on the side.

Serves 4 to 6.

Linguine Fini with Walnut Sauce

- 1 pound linguine fini
- 2 cups walnuts
- 1 cup pignoli
- 2 cloves garlic
- 2 tablespoons chopped fresh parsley
- 2 tablespoons butter, melted
- 2 tablespoons oil
- 1 cup ricotta cheese
- 2 tablespoons water
- 1 teaspoon salt
- ¼ teaspoon freshly ground black pepper
- ½ cup freshly grated Romano cheese

Cook the pasta according to package directions until al dente; drain.

While the pasta is cooking, combine the remaining ingredients except the Romano cheese in a blender or food processor. (You will probably have to do this in batches.) Blend until creamy.

Place the pasta in a warmed deep bowl. Pour the sauce over the pasta, toss to blend, and sprinkle with Romano cheese.

Serves 4 to 6.

Linguine with Eggplant Sauce

2 tablespoons butter
2 tablespoons oil
2 medium onions, finely chopped
2 cloves garlic, minced
1 medium (about 1½ pounds) eggplant, peeled and cut into cubes
1 28-ounce can plum tomatoes
3 small carrots, finely chopped
1 teaspoon salt
¼ teaspoon dried basil
¼ cup pignoli
1 pound linguine
½ cup freshly grated Parmesan cheese

Melt the butter in the oil in a heavy 10- to 12-inch skillet over medium heat. Add the onions, garlic, and eggplant. Sauté until the onions are transparent. Add the tomatoes, crushing them in your hand as you add them, and the liquid from the can. Stir in the carrots, salt, and basil. Bring the mixture to a boil, lower the heat, and simmer, uncovered, for about 1½ hours. Stir from time to time to avoid burning. Just before serving, mix in the pignoli.

When the sauce is almost ready, cook the pasta according to package directions until al dente; drain. Put the pasta into a warmed deep bowl and add the sauce; mix gently. Sprinkle with the cheese and serve.

Serves 4 to 6.

Linguine with John's White Clam Sauce

4 tablespoons olive oil
4 cloves garlic, minced
2 tablespoons chopped fresh parsley
1 tablespoon chopped fresh basil leaves, or 1 teaspoon dried basil
¼ teaspoon freshly ground black pepper
⅛ teaspoon dried oregano
12 littleneck clams, well scrubbed
2 8-ounce cans minced clams
1 pound linguine

Heat the oil in a heavy skillet that will hold the clams in one layer. Add the garlic, parsley, basil, pepper, oregano, and littleneck clams. Cook over medium-high heat, shaking the pan occasionally, until the clams open. (Discard any that don't open.) Remove the clams from the pan and add the 2 cans of clams with their liquid. Bring to a boil and cook, stirring, for 5 minutes.

While the sauce is cooking, cook the pasta according to package directions until al dente; drain. Put the pasta on a warmed platter, pour the clam sauce over it, and top with the clams in shells.

Serves 4 to 6.

Linguine with Asparagus

1 pound fresh asparagus
1 pound linguine
1 teaspoon salt
¼ teaspoon freshly ground
    black pepper
3 tablespoons olive oil
    Freshly grated Romano
    cheese

Clean the asparagus and snap off the tough ends; cut into 1-inch pieces.

Cook the pasta according to package directions until al dente; drain. Meanwhile, cook the asparagus in boiling, salted water until it is tender but still crisp, about 4 minutes; drain.

Put the pasta into a warmed deep bowl with the asparagus. Sprinkle with the salt and pepper. Add the olive oil and mix well. Toss the pasta with 2 or 3 tablespoons of grated cheese. Serve hot with additional cheese on the side.

Serves 4 to 6.

NOTE: Instead of fresh asparagus, you may use 1 10-ounce package frozen asparagus tips, thawed and cooked for just a moment or two.

Mama D's Fettuccine Alfredo

1 pound fettuccine
8 tablespoons butter
¼ pound mushrooms, sliced
½ teaspoon salt
¼ teaspoon freshly ground
    black pepper
¼ teaspoon dried oregano
1 teaspoon minced garlic
¼ cup freshly grated Romano
    cheese
¼ cup freshly shredded
    mozzarella cheese

Preheat the oven to 375 degrees.

Cook the fettuccine according to package directions. While the pasta is cooking, melt the butter in a skillet. Add the mushrooms, salt, pepper, oregano, and garlic; cook until the mushrooms are heated through.

When the fettuccine is just al dente, drain and place it in a shallow baking dish. Toss with the Romano cheese and then stir in the butter mixture. Sprinkle with the mozzarella cheese and bake until the cheese is melted but not browned, about 5 minutes. Serve hot.

Serves 4 to 6.

Baked Eggplant Lasagna

1 large (about 2½ pounds)
  eggplant
1 teaspoon salt
¼ teaspoon freshly ground
  black pepper
¼ teaspoon dried oregano
½ teaspoon minced garlic
1 cup all-purpose flour
2 eggs
2 tablespoons water
  Oil for frying
2½ cups Tomato Sauce (see
  page 79)
½ pound lasagna noodles,
  cooked, rinsed in cold
  water, and drained
1 cup freshly grated Romano
  cheese
2 cups ricotta cheese
2 cups freshly shredded
  mozzarella cheese

Preheat the oven to 375 degrees.

Peel the eggplant and cut lengthwise into ¼-inch-thick slices. Mix the salt, pepper, oregano, and garlic with the flour. Beat the eggs with the water. Dip the eggplant slices in the egg mixture then dredge them in the seasoned flour. Add enough oil to a heavy 10- to 12-inch skillet to cover the bottom of the pan. Heat over medium-high heat. Fry the eggplant slices in batches until golden brown on both sides. Drain on paper towels.

Pour ¼ inch hot water into the bottom of a 13½-by-9½-by-2-inch baking dish. Add ½ cup of the Tomato Sauce. Place a layer of lasagna noodles over the sauce and cover with a layer of eggplant slices. Sprinkle with about 4 tablespoons of the Romano cheese. Dab with 1 cup of the ricotta, and sprinkle with ⅔ cup of the mozzarella. Repeat, ending with a final layer of lasagna noodles. Pour enough of the sauce over the top to cover generously. Sprinkle with the remaining Romano and mozzarella. Cover the baking dish tightly with aluminum foil. Bake for 45 minutes.

Serves 4 to 6.

Fettuccine with Creamed Spinach

- 2 tablespoons butter
- 1½ pounds spinach, washed, cooked, and shredded
- 3 tablespoons butter
- 6 slices bacon, cut into small pieces
- 4 tablespoons all-purpose flour
- 1¼ cups milk, heated
- 1 teaspoon salt
- ¼ teaspoon freshly ground black pepper
- ½ teaspoon minced garlic
- 1 small onion, minced
- 1 pound fettuccine
- ⅔ cup freshly grated Romano cheese

Preheat the oven to 375 degrees.

Melt the 2 tablespoons butter in a heavy 10- to 12-inch skillet and add the spinach. Cook, stirring, until blended. Set aside.

Melt the 3 tablespoons butter in a saucepan. Fry the bacon in the butter until it is almost crisp. Remove with a slotted spoon and reserve. Blend the flour into the bacon drippings and butter. Gradually add the milk, stirring to dissolve any lumps. Simmer, stirring occasionally, until the sauce is smooth and thickened. Add the salt, pepper, garlic, and onion. Add the spinach and simmer 5 minutes more.

While the sauce is simmering, cook the pasta according to package directions just until al dente; drain. Place the pasta in a shallow baking dish. Sprinkle with the cheese.

Pour the sauce over the pasta and sprinkle the bacon over the top. Bake until the ingredients are hot and bubbling, about 5 minutes.

Serves 4 to 6.

Cavatelli with Lima Bean Sauce

- 1 tablespoon butter
- 1 tablespoon olive oil
- ½ pound bacon, cut into pieces
- 2 small onions, finely chopped
- 2 cloves garlic, minced
- 1 pound lima beans
- 1 pound cavatelli
- ½ cup freshly grated Parmesan cheese

Melt the butter in the oil in a heavy 8-inch skillet over medium heat. Add the bacon and fry, stirring as needed, until the bacon is crisp. Remove the bacon from the skillet with a slotted spoon and reserve. Add the onions and garlic to the skillet and sauté until the onions are transparent. Add the bacon and lima beans (drained, if canned); simmer, uncovered, for 10 minutes.

Cook the pasta according to package directions until al dente; drain. Put the pasta into a warmed deep bowl and stir in the lima bean mixture. Add the cheese and mix well. Serve hot.

Serves 4 to 6.

Bow Ties with Eggplant Meatballs

....

Eggplant Meatballs (recipe follows)
4 cups Tomato Sauce (see page 79)
1 pound bow ties
½ cup freshly grated Romano cheese

Prepare the meatballs and heat the tomato sauce. When the sauce is hot, add the meatballs. Cook the pasta according to package directions until al dente; drain. Put the pasta onto a warmed platter, stir in about 2 cups of the sauce, and top with the meatballs. Sprinkle with the Romano cheese. Serve hot with the remaining sauce on the side.

Serves 4 to 6.

Eggplant Meatballs

1 medium (about 1½ pounds) eggplant, peeled and diced
1 pound ground beef
3 slices stale bread, soaked in water, and squeezed dry
3 eggs
½ cup freshly grated Romano cheese
¼ cup chopped fresh parsley
¼ teaspoon fennel seeds
¼ teaspoon freshly ground black pepper
1 teaspoon salt
¼ teaspoon dried thyme
½ teaspoon minced garlic

Preheat the oven to 375 degrees.

Cook the eggplant in boiling water until soft. Drain the eggplant and put it into a large bowl with the beef. Tear the bread into pieces and add to the bowl with the remaining ingredients. Mix gently, but thoroughly, with your hands.

With lightly oiled hands, roll the mixture into balls, each about the size of a golf ball. Place the balls in a greased, shallow baking pan and bake until the balls are browned and cooked through, about 30 to 35 minutes.

Makes about 16 meatballs.

Ravioli

∙∙∙∙∙∙∙∙∙∙∙

¾ pound ground beef
¾ pound ricotta cheese
3 eggs, beaten
1½ cups freshly grated Parmesan cheese
Pinch of freshly ground nutmeg
Salt and freshly ground black pepper, to taste
Ravioli Dough (recipe follows)
6 quarts water
1 tablespoon salt
Tomato Sauce (see page 79)
Freshly grated Parmesan cheese

Mix the ground beef, ricotta, eggs, 1 cup of the Parmesan cheese, nutmeg, salt, and pepper together in a bowl; set aside. Make the Ravioli Dough.

Divide the dough into 5 sections and roll out each section into a very thin rectangle. Cut the rectangles into strips, each about 3-by-10 inches. Drop 1 teaspoon of filling on a strip at 2-inch intervals. Mold another strip of dough on top and cut with a ravioli cutter into 2-by-2-inch squares. (You may use a knife to cut it; press the edges with a fork to seal.) Place the ravioli on a lightly floured board and cover with a clean cloth.

Bring 6 quarts water and 1 tablespoon salt to a rolling boil in a large pot. Add the ravioli and cook until tender, 8 to 10 minutes; drain in a colander. Before serving, heat the Tomato Sauce, pour it over the ravioli, and sprinkle with the remaining grated Parmesan cheese.

Makes 24 ravioli.

Ravioli Dough

3 cups all-purpose flour
3 eggs, beaten
1 tablespoon oil
1 scant tablespoon salt
Water

Place the flour in a bowl. Make a well in the center and drop in the eggs, oil, and salt. Add the water a little at a time (enough to make a smooth dough) and knead on a floured board until the dough is smooth and elastic. Invert a large bowl over the dough and let it sit for 5 minutes.

Papa V's Ditalini and Red Kidney Beans

1 pound ditalini
3 tablespoons olive oil
1 large clove garlic, minced
  Pinch of crushed red pepper
⅛ teaspoon dried oregano
⅛ teaspoon dried basil
1 20-ounce can red kidney
  beans
  Salt to taste
  Freshly grated Parmesan or
  Romano cheese

Cook the pasta according to package directions.

While the pasta is cooking, heat the oil in a heavy 8-inch skillet over medium heat. Add the garlic, red pepper, oregano, and basil. Sauté until the garlic is golden. Add the beans and their liquid to the skillet and heat almost to a boil. Season with salt to taste.

When the pasta is just al dente, drain and put it into a warmed deep bowl. Add the contents of the skillet and mix thoroughly. If the mixture is too dry for your taste, add a tablespoon or two of olive oil. Serve with grated cheese on the side.

Serves 4 to 6.

N O T E : This recipe was given to me by Vincent Picarello. I tried it with canned fava beans, too, and it's good either way.

Paglia e Fieno (Straw and Hay)

3 tablespoons butter
3 tablespoons olive oil
2 cloves garlic, minced
½ pound green noodles
½ pound wide fettuccine
1 cup ricotta cheese, at room
  temperature
¼ cup freshly grated Romano
  cheese
1 teaspoon salt
¼ teaspoon freshly ground
  black pepper

Melt the butter in the oil in a heavy skillet over medium heat. Add the garlic and sauté until the garlic is golden. Set aside.

Cook the pastas in two separate pots according to package directions until al dente; drain. Combine the pastas in a warmed deep bowl. Add the butter and oil mixture, the cheeses, and the salt and pepper. Stir gently to combine and serve hot.

Serves 4 to 6.

Bucatini with Anchovy, Garlic, and Oil Sauce

2 tablespoons butter
½ cup olive oil
5 cloves garlic, minced
1 2-ounce can anchovy fillets
¼ teaspoon freshly ground black pepper
1 pound bucatini
½ cup freshly grated Romano cheese

Melt the butter in the oil in a heavy 8-inch skillet. Add the garlic and sauté until the garlic is golden. Add the anchovies, with the oil from the can, to the skillet. Sprinkle with the pepper. Reduce the heat and cook slowly, uncovered, for about 30 minutes.

Cook the pasta according to package directions until al dente; drain. Place the pasta on a warmed platter and pour the sauce over it; stir gently. Sprinkle with the cheese and serve.

Serves 4 to 6.

Riccini with Zucchini in Basil Sauce

1 pound riccini
4 tablespoons olive oil
3 medium zucchini, sliced into ¼-inch rounds
2 tablespoons butter
3 tablespoons all-purpose flour
2 cups milk
½ cup finely chopped fresh basil leaves
1 teaspoon salt
2 eggs, well beaten
½ cup freshly grated Romano cheese

Cook the pasta according to package directions until al dente; drain.

While the pasta is cooking, heat the oil in a heavy 10- to 12-inch skillet over medium heat. Add the zucchini slices and fry until lightly colored. Remove the zucchini to a large serving dish and drain the oil from the pan. Melt the butter in the pan. Stir in the flour and add the milk gradually, stirring to dissolve any lumps. Add the basil and salt and stir to mix. Remove the pan from the heat and stir in the eggs and cheese.

Add the pasta to the zucchini and stir in the sauce. Serve hot.

Serves 4 to 6.

Vegetables

Baked Rosemary Potatoes

- 8 small potatoes, peeled
- ½ cup oil
- 1 teaspoon salt
- ¼ teaspoon freshly ground black pepper
- 1 teaspoon minced garlic
- 1 teaspoon dried rosemary

Preheat the oven to 375 degrees.

Combine all ingredients and toss together. Put them into a greased baking dish and bake until golden brown, about 50 to 60 minutes.

Serves 4 to 6.

Mashed Turnips

- 6 to 8 medium turnips
- 2 tablespoons butter
- ½ teaspoon salt
- ¼ teaspoon freshly ground black pepper
- ¼ cup freshly grated Romano cheese
- ¼ cup milk
- 1 tablespoon butter

Peel the turnips. Cook them in boiling salted water until fork tender, about 20 to 25 minutes. Drain and mash them as you would potatoes. Add the remaining ingredients and mash again. If the turnips have cooled, reheat them in the oven for a few minutes. Melt 1 tablespoon more of butter in the center of the turnips, turn them into a serving bowl, and serve hot.

Serves 4.

Zucchini alla Romano Casserole

- 6 small zucchini, sliced into ⅓-inch-thick rounds
- 2 onions, chopped
- 2 stalks celery, diced
- 2 cloves garlic, minced
- 2 green peppers, diced
- 1 cup sliced mushrooms
- ½ teaspoon freshly ground black pepper
  Salt, to taste
- ¼ cup freshly grated Romano cheese
- ¼ cup oil
- 3 fresh tomatoes or 1 cup canned tomatoes, crushed
- ¼ cup freshly and coarsely grated mozzarella cheese

Preheat the oven to 375 degrees.

Arrange the zucchini in a greased casserole. Add the onions, celery, garlic, green peppers, mushrooms, pepper, salt, and Romano cheese. Pour the oil over the vegetables and toss gently. Spoon the crushed tomatoes over the top of the vegetables and sprinkle with mozzarella cheese. Bake, covered, for 1 hour. Serve hot.

Serves 4.

Parsnip Fritters

4 to 6 parsnips
1 cup all-purpose flour
½ teaspoon baking powder
Salt, to taste
Freshly ground black pepper,
to taste
¼ cup freshly grated Romano
cheese
⅔ cup water
2 eggs
Vegetable shortening for
frying

Wash, peel, and dice the parsnips. Place the parsnips in a saucepan with water to cover and simmer for 6 or 7 minutes. Drain, dry, and put in a bowl and mash. Add the flour, baking powder, salt, pepper, and cheese. Mix in the water and eggs. Beat until the mixture has the consistency of pancake batter. Heat the shortening in a skillet. Drop the batter by teaspoonfuls into the hot shortening and fry until golden brown on all sides.

Serves 6 (12 to 15 fritters).

You don't need a fancy electric deepfryer. Heat oil to a 1-inch depth in a heavy frying pan. Test the temperature of the oil by throwing a bread cube into the pan. If the cube rapidly fries to a golden brown, the oil is hot enough for deep-frying.

Scalloped Eggplant

2 medium eggplants, peeled
1 cup milk
4 tablespoon butter
4 hard-boiled eggs, peeled
and chopped
1½ cups bread crumbs
1 clove garlic, minced
Salt
⅛ teaspoon dried oregano
½ teaspoon freshly ground
black pepper
2 green peppers, diced
2 small onions, finely
chopped
½ cup freshly grated Romano
cheese

Preheat the oven to 350 degrees.

Cut the eggplants into 1-inch cubes. Place the cubes in a saucepan and cover with water. Bring to a boil, cook the eggplant about 7 minutes, and drain. Scald the milk, add the butter, and set aside. Mix together all the remaining ingredients except the Romano cheese and toss gently with the eggplant. Put the eggplant mixture into a casserole and pour the scalded milk over it. Sprinkle with the Romano cheese. Bake, uncovered, for about 40 minutes.

Serves 4 to 6.

Broccoli al Siciliano

1 bunch fresh broccoli
1 large onion, sliced into thin rings
½ cup sliced olives
½ cup freshly grated Parmesan cheese
Salt, to taste
Freshly ground black pepper
1 teaspoon minced garlic
⅓ cup oil
½ cup dry red or white wine

Preheat the oven to 375 degrees.

Clean and wash the broccoli. Cut the broccoli into small pieces and place in a greased baking dish. Arrange the onions and olives over the broccoli. Sprinkle with the cheese. Season with salt, pepper, and garlic. Sprinkle the oil and wine over the top. Cover the baking dish with aluminum foil and bake until the broccoli is tender, about 20 to 30 minutes.

Serves 4 to 6.

Collards

¼ cup oil
2 onions, diced
2 cloves garlic, minced
3 or 4 fresh tomatoes, crushed
2 cups water
1 teaspoon salt
¼ teaspoon freshly ground black pepper
1½ pounds collards
3 carrots, sliced
3 medium potatoes, peeled and cubed

Heat the oil in a 4-quart saucepan. Add the onions and garlic and sauté until the onions are transparent. Add the tomatoes, water, salt, and pepper.

Wash the collards thoroughly and cut up the tender leaves, discarding the tough stems and the midribs of the leaves. Add the carrots, potatoes, and collards to the saucepan. Simmer, covered, over low heat until the potatoes and carrots are tender, about 30 to 35 minutes.

Serves 4.

Spinach alla Piemontese

1½ pounds spinach
4 tablespoons butter
1 tablespoon oil
1 clove garlic, crushed
2 tablespoons finely diced anchovy fillets
Salt, to taste
¼ teaspoon freshly ground black pepper

Wash the spinach and put it in a 2-quart pot with about ½ cup water. Cook the spinach, covered, over low heat until tender, about 5 to 7 minutes. Drain well. Melt the butter in the oil in a 2-quart pot. Add the garlic and sauté until the garlic is lightly browned. Add the spinach, anchovies, salt, and pepper. Mix well and serve.

Serves 4 to 6.

Zucchini with Anchovy Sauce

¼ cup oil
5 zucchini, sliced
2 cloves garlic, minced
2 tablespoons chopped fresh parsley
¼ teaspoon salt
⅛ teaspoon freshly ground black pepper
⅛ teaspoon dried oregano
4 anchovy fillets, finely diced
1 tablespoon vinegar

Heat the oil in a skillet and sauté the zucchini for 2 or 3 minutes. Add the garlic, parsley, salt, pepper, oregano, and anchovies. Stir well and cook until the zucchini is tender. Add the vinegar. Cook, stirring, for 3 to 5 minutes and serve.

Serves 4.

Swiss Chard with Bacon

2 pounds fresh Swiss chard
½ cup water
¼ cup oil
½ pound bacon, chopped
1 large onion, chopped
2 cloves garlic, minced
1 cup sliced mushrooms
¼ teaspoon freshly ground black pepper
¼ cup freshly grated Romano cheese
1 cup bread crumbs

Cut the Swiss chard from the stems. Discard the stems; wash and shred the leaves; Put the chard leaves in a saucepan with the water, bring to a boil, and cook for 10 minutes. In a skillet heat the oil and bacon. Add the onion, garlic, mushrooms, and pepper. Sauté until the onions are transparent. Pour the bacon-onion mixture over the Swiss chard. Add the cheese and bread crumbs and simmer for 10 minutes. Serve hot.

Serves 6.

Swiss Chard

1 pound fresh Swiss chard
½ cup water
¼ cup olive oil
2 cloves garlic, minced
  Salt, to taste
¼ teaspoon dried oregano
¼ teaspoon freshly ground
  black pepper

Wash the chard. Cut the stalks into two-inch sections and cut up the leaves if they are large. Put the chard in a saucepan with the water, bring to a boil, and cook for about 10 minutes. Heat the oil in a skillet and sauté the garlic until it is lightly browned. Add the chard and seasonings. Simmer together for about 5 minutes and serve.

Serves 4.

Kale

1½ pounds kale
   Salt, to taste
½ teaspoon freshly ground
  black pepper
4 tablespoons butter

Select the tender leaves of the kale; wash well. Cook the leaves slowly in 1 inch of boiling water until tender, about 10 to 15 minutes. Add the remaining ingredients, toss gently, and serve.

Serves 4.

Asparagus, Milan Style

1 pound fresh asparagus,
  trimmed of tough ends
3 eggs
  Pinch of salt
¼ teaspoon freshly ground
  black pepper
1 clove garlic, minced
½ cup freshly grated Romano
  cheese

Preheat the oven to 350 degrees.
  Cook the asparagus in boiling, salted water until barely tender, about 5 minutes; drain. Put the asparagus in a buttered baking dish.
  Beat the eggs with the salt, pepper, and garlic. Pour the egg mixture over the asparagus. Sprinkle with the cheese. Bake, uncovered, until the eggs are set, about 20 minutes.

Serves 3 to 4.

Fried Eggplant

1 large eggplant
Salt, to taste
2 eggs, beaten
2 tablespoons water
1½ cups bread crumbs
¼ cup freshly grated Romano cheese
2 tablespoons minced parsley
Salt, to taste
½ teaspoon freshly ground black pepper
¼ teaspoon dried oregano
2 cloves garlic, minced
Oil for frying

Peel the eggplant and cut it lengthwise into thin strips. Sprinkle with a little salt. Put the strips in a single layer on a plate and cover with another plate. Weigh down the second plate to press out the juice. Set aside for 1 hour. Squeeze the eggplant dry. Beat the eggs with the water; set aside. Thoroughly combine all of the remaining ingredients, except the oil. Dip the eggplant slices into the egg and then into the bread-crumb mixture. Fry the slices in hot oil until golden brown, about 2 minutes on each side.

Serves 4.

Endive-Potato Stew

¼ cup oil
2 cloves garlic, minced
2 onions, diced
1 6-ounce can tomato paste
6 ounces water (using the tomato paste can as a measure)
½ teaspoon salt
½ teaspoon freshly ground black pepper
6 potatoes, peeled and cubed
1½ pounds fresh endive, sliced
¼ cup freshly grated Romano cheese

Heat the oil in a Dutch oven. Sauté the garlic and onions until the onions are transparent. Add the tomato paste and water and simmer slowly for 10 minutes. Then add the salt, pepper, and cubed potatoes. Cook for another 10 minutes. Add the endive. Cover and simmer the stew until the potatoes are tender, about 1 hour. Add the grated cheese and salt and pepper to taste.

Serves 4.

Lima Beans with Linguine

      1/4 cup oil
        1 small onion, finely chopped
        2 cloves garlic, minced
        1 teaspoon salt
      1/4 teaspoon freshly ground
          black pepper
        2 cups canned tomatoes,
          crushed
        2 cups water
    2 1/2 cups lima beans, canned or
          frozen
        1 pound linguine
      1/2 cup freshly grated Romano
          cheese

Heat the oil in a heavy skillet and sauté the onion and garlic until the onion is transparent. Add the seasonings, crushed tomatoes, and water. Simmer slowly for 2 hours. Add the lima beans to the sauce for the last 30 minutes of cooking. Add the linguine to boiling, salted water and cook according to package directions until al dente; drain. Put the linguine on a warmed platter, pour the bean sauce over it, and sprinkle with the cheese.

Serves 4 to 6.

Dandelion Stew

        4 cups dandelion greens
      1/4 cup oil
        2 cloves garlic, minced
        2 onions, diced
        4 carrots, cooked and cut into
          chunks
        4 medium potatoes, peeled,
          parboiled, and cubed
        1 cup crushed tomatoes, fresh
          or canned
          Salt, to taste
      1/4 teaspoon freshly ground
          black pepper
      1/8 teaspoon dried oregano

Pick the dandelions in the spring of the year before their flowers appear. Wash them carefully in several changes of water to remove any sand and dirt embedded in the leaves. Cook the greens in 4 cups of boiling water for 15 minutes. Drain, reserving 2 cups of the cooking liquid.

Heat the oil in a heavy saucepan. Sauté the garlic and onions until the onions are transparent. Add the carrots, potatoes, dandelion greens, and the 2 cups reserved dandelion cooking liquid. Stir in the tomatoes and the seasonings. Cook slowly, covered, for 30 minutes.

Serves 4 to 6.

Dandelion Greens

2 pounds dandelion greens
3 cloves garlic, minced
1½ teaspoons salt
¼ teaspoon freshly ground pepper
½ cup vegetable oil
½ cup freshly grated Romano cheese

Wash the greens thoroughly. Place the greens in a large kettle of boiling, salted water and cook until tender, 10 to 15 minutes; drain. Return the greens to the kettle and add the garlic, salt, pepper, oil, and cheese. Toss lightly.

Serves 4.

Cooks are not born—they're made. When I was a young bride, I moved to Chicago where my husband's family lived. His family had so many excellent cooks that I was actually ashamed to ask my sisters-in-law to help me. Every day I'd go to a different person I knew so they wouldn't think I was that dumb. I'd say, "What are you cooking today?" And they'd say, "Oh, I'm having zucchini." "Well," I'd say, "tell me. I'd like some. What do I do?" And that was the way I learned to cook. Who'd ever know that so many years later I'd have a restaurant and make use of all those little things these ladies taught me?

Brussels Sprouts

1¼ pounds fresh Brussels sprouts
1 teaspoon salt
¼ teaspoon freshly ground black pepper
2 cloves garlic, minced
¼ cup oil
¼ cup freshly grated Parmesan cheese

Thoroughly wash the Brussels sprouts in cold water and remove any discolored leaves. Cook the sprouts in a small amount of boiling, salted water until they are just tender, about 5 to 10 minutes; drain. Put the sprouts in a serving dish and add the salt, pepper, and garlic. Drizzle the oil over the top and sprinkle with the cheese.

Serves 4.

Fava Beans

1 pound fava beans
½ teaspoon baking soda
¼ cup oil
2 cloves garlic, minced
2 onions, finely chopped
1 teaspoon salt
¼ teaspoon freshly ground black pepper

Wash the fava beans and soak them overnight in clear water. Discard the soaking water.

Bring water to a boil in a heavy 4-quart saucepan. Add the fava beans and baking soda. Cook over low heat until the beans are tender, about 1 hour. Heat the oil in a skillet; sauté the garlic and onions until the onions are transparent. Add the salt and pepper and stir. Pour the onion mixture over the beans and serve.

Serves 6.

Sautéed Zucchini

    4 medium zucchini, thinly
      sliced
    3 tablespoons olive oil
    1 clove garlic, minced
    3 tablespoons wine vinegar
    3 tablespoons water
    3 anchovy fillets
      Salt, to taste
 1/8 teaspoon freshly ground
      black pepper
      Freshly grated Parmesan
      cheese

Heat the oil in a skillet. Add the garlic and sauté until the garlic is golden. Add the zucchini and cover the pan for 3 to 5 minutes. Add the vinegar, water, and anchovies. Simmer for 10 to 15 minutes. Add the salt and pepper, sprinkle with the cheese, and serve.

Serves 4 to 6.

Baked Zucchini with Mozzarella Cheese

 1/4 cup oil
    2 small onions, finely chopped
    1 teaspoon garlic, minced
    1 6-ounce can tomato paste
    6 ounces water (using the
      tomato paste can as a
      measure)
    2 ripe tomatoes, peeled and
      coarsely chopped
      Salt
 1/2 teaspoon freshly ground
      black pepper
    1 teaspoon dried basil
    6 small zucchini, cut into
      1/4-inch-thick slices
 1/2 pound mozzarella cheese,
      sliced
    4 anchovy fillets (optional), cut
      into pieces

Heat the oil in a saucepan and sauté the onions and garlic until the onions are transparent. Add the tomato paste, water, tomatoes, salt, pepper, and basil; simmer until the sauce is slightly reduced, about 20 minutes.

Preheat the oven to 350 degrees.

Cover the bottom of an oiled baking dish with the zucchini slices. Pour the tomato sauce over the zucchini and cover with some slices of cheese. Repeat the layers until you have used all the zucchini, ending with the sauce and cheese. Arrange the anchovy fillets on top and bake until the cheese is melted and bubbly, about 20 minutes.

Serves 4 to 6.

Zucchini with Onions

1/4 cup olive oil
3 medium zucchini, thinly sliced
2 small onions, thinly sliced
Salt
Freshly ground black pepper
1 clove garlic, minced
2 tablespoons wine vinegar (optional)
2 tablespoons freshly grated Parmesan cheese

Heat the oil in a skillet. Add the zucchini and onions and sauté slowly until the onions are transparent. Add the salt, pepper, and garlic and cook until the zucchini is tender. Stir in the wine vinegar (it adds a little more flavor). Before serving, sprinkle with cheese.

Serves 4.

Italian Zucchini Chops

12 ounces beer
1 egg
4 tablespoons all-purpose flour
1 teaspoon salt
1/4 teaspoon freshly ground black pepper
1/2 teaspoon minced garlic
1/2 cup freshly grated Romano cheese
6 small zucchini, thinly sliced
Oil for frying

To make the batter, pour the beer in a large bowl and add the egg, flour, salt, pepper, garlic, and cheese; mix well. Let the mixture stand for 5 minutes.

Heat 1 inch of cooking oil in a large skillet. Dip the zucchini in the batter. Fry each slice on both sides to a golden brown. Drain on paper towels.

Serves 4 to 6.

Peel large zucchini; they're usually a little tough. The big ones are good sliced, dipped in egg and then in flour seasoned with the SPOGs (salt, pepper, oregano, garlic) and a little grated Parmesan cheese, then fried. They're really delicious.

Zucchini Fritters

- 2 medium zucchini, sliced paper-thin
- 1 cup all-purpose flour
- 2 eggs, beaten
  Salt
  Freshly ground black pepper
- 1 clove garlic, minced
- ¼ cup water
- ¼ cup freshly grated Parmesan cheese
- 1 cup vegetable oil

Combine the zucchini, flour, eggs, salt, pepper, garlic, water and cheese; mix thoroughly. (The mixture will be the consistency of pancake batter.) Heat the oil in a skillet. When hot, drop the batter by tablespoonfuls into the oil and fry until golden brown on all sides. Drain on paper towels.

Serves 4 to 6.

Green Beans, Potatoes, and Zucchini

- 1 pound green beans
- 2 medium potatoes, peeled and diced
- ½ cup vegetable or olive oil
- 1 onion, sliced
- 2 cloves garlic, minced
- 2 medium zucchini, sliced ½-inch thick
- ½ cup Tomato Sauce (optional) (see page 79)
  Salt
  Freshly ground black pepper
- ½ cup freshly grated Romano cheese

Remove and discard the tips from the beans; cut the beans in half. Cook the potatoes in boiling water for 5 to 6 minutes: add the beans and cook 3 minutes more; drain. In a large skillet heat the oil. Sauté the onion and garlic until the onion is transparent. Add the zucchini, Tomato Sauce, salt, pepper, beans, and potatoes. Cook, covered, over low heat, for 15 minutes. Sprinkle with the grated cheese and serve.

Serves 4 to 6.

Croquettes

3 cups mashed potatoes

¼ cup freshly grated Parmesan
cheese

½ cup all-purpose flour

½ cup bread crumbs

3 eggs, beaten

2 cloves garlic, minced
Salt
Freshly ground black pepper
Oil for frying

Mix all the ingredients except the oil. Shape
into croquettes. Heat 1 inch of oil in a 6- to
8-inch skillet. When the oil is hot enough, fry
the croquettes until golden brown on all sides.
Serve hot.

Serves 6 to 8.

Baked Potatoes
with Mozzarella Cheese

4 baking potatoes
Oil
Salt
Freshly ground black pepper

½ cup milk

2 tablespoons butter

¼ cup freshly grated Parmesan
cheese

4 slices mozzarella cheese

Preheat the oven to 375 degrees.

Thoroughly wash and oil each potato.
Bake until the potatoes seem tender when
tested with a fork, about 1 hour. Remove the
potatoes from the oven, but do not turn the
oven off. Cut a thin slice lengthwise from each
potato and scoop out the insides into a mixing
bowl, leaving a thin shell. Reserve the shells.
Mash the potatoes well, adding salt and pepper. Add a little milk and butter and 2 tablespoons of the Parmesan cheese; beat until
fluffy. Fill the potato shells with the mashed
potato mixture and sprinkle with the remaining Parmesan cheese. Put a thin slice of mozzarella cheese on each potato. Place the
potatoes on a baking sheet and bake until the
cheese melts, about 10 minutes.

Serves 4.

Baked Stuffed Potatoes

4 large potatoes, baked until
tender

¼ cup chopped onion

1 teaspoon salt

½ teaspoon freshly ground
black pepper

1 teaspoon minced garlic

¼ cup freshly grated Romano
cheese

1 egg

2 slices ham, diced

8 thin slices mozzarella cheese

Preheat the oven to 375 degrees.

Thoroughly wash each potato. Bake until
the potatoes seem tender when tested with a
fork, about 1 hour. Remove the potatoes from

the oven and cut them in half lengthwise. Scoop out the insides, leaving the potato skins intact. Mash the potatoes with the onion, salt, pepper, garlic, Romano cheese, egg, and ham. Fill the potato skins with the mixture and bake for 12 minutes. Place a slice of mozzarella over each potato half and bake until the cheese is melted and bubbly, about 10 minutes more.

Serves 8.

Romano Fried Potatoes
....

¼ cup bread crumbs
¼ cup freshly grated Romano
    cheese
    Pinch of salt
¼ teaspoon freshly ground
    black pepper
 1 clove garlic, minced
    Oil for deep frying
 4 large Idaho potatoes, peeled
    and cut into lengthwise strips
 2 eggs, beaten

Preheat the oven to 350 degrees.

Mix the bread crumbs, cheese, salt, pepper, and garlic. Heat the oil to 375 degrees. Dip the potato strips into the beaten eggs, then into the bread-crumb mixture. Fry until golden brown on all sides. Put the strips in a baking dish and bake until tender, at least 30 minutes. Serve hot.

Serves 4 to 6.

Gnocchi
....

 6 large potatoes, unpeeled
 2 eggs, beaten
 2 tablespoons oil or butter
 1 teaspoon salt
½ cup freshly grated Parmesan
    cheese
 1 to 1½ cups all-purpose flour
    Garlic Butter (recipe follows)
    or
    Bolognese Tomato Sauce
    (see page 77)
    Freshly grated Parmesan
    cheese

Boil the potatoes in their skins until tender; peel. Mash the potatoes or put them through a potato ricer. Blend in the eggs, oil, salt, and cheese. Then add the flour, a little at a time, until thoroughly blended in. Turn the dough out onto a floured board and knead lightly; form the dough into 1-inch-thick ropes. Cut each rope into pieces ¾-inch long. Cook in boiling salted water until the gnocchi rise to the top of the water. Cook a little longer, about 2 to 3 minutes; drain. Pour the Garlic Butter over the gnocchi and toss lightly, or cover with Bolognese Tomato Sauce. Spoon all onto a serving platter and sprinkle with cheese. Serve hot.

Serves 4 to 6.

Garlic Butter

    Salt and pepper, to taste
 1 clove garlic, mashed
16 tablespoons butter, melted

Add the salt, pepper, and garlic to the butter.

Italian Carrots

1 pound carrots, unpeeled
1 green pepper, julienned
1 onion, finely chopped
1 teaspoon salt
¼ teaspoon freshly ground
 black pepper
1 teaspoon minced garlic
3 teaspoons olive oil
1 teaspoon wine vinegar

Thoroughly wash the carrots, cut them diagonally, and cook in boiling water until just tender, about 10 minutes; drain. When the carrots have cooled, combine them with the remaining ingredients. Refrigerate for 2 hours before serving.

Serves 4.

Peppers and Potatoes

¼ cup oil
2 small onions, minced
3 cloves garlic, minced
6 green peppers, julienned
6 medium potatoes, peeled and
 sliced
1 teaspoon salt
½ teaspoon freshly ground
 black pepper
1 cup Tomato Sauce (see page
 79)
¼ cup freshly grated Romano
 cheese

Heat the oil in a skillet and sauté the onions and garlic until they are soft. Add the green peppers, potatoes, salt, pepper, and tomato sauce. Cook over low heat until the potatoes are tender, about 30 to 40 minutes. Place all on a platter, sprinkle with the cheese, and serve hot.

Serves 4.

Stuffed Mushrooms

1 pound fresh mushrooms
5 slices bacon
½ cup minced onion
8 ounces cream cheese,
 softened
2 teaspoons minced parsley
1 teaspoon salt
½ teaspoon freshly ground
 black pepper
½ teaspoon finely chopped
 fresh basil
2 cloves garlic, minced

Preheat the oven to 425 degrees.
 Wash the mushrooms. Leave the mushroom caps whole; remove and mince the stems. Fry the bacon until it is crisp; remove it with a slotted spoon and crumble. Sauté the onion in the bacon fat until it is transparent. Place the cream cheese in a bowl and combine with the mushroom stems, bacon, onion, parsley, salt, pepper, basil, and garlic. Stuff the mushroom caps with the mixture. Place the filled caps on a greased cookie sheet and bake for 8 to 10 minutes.

Serves 4.

Peas with Prosciutto

2 tablespoons butter
¼ pound prosciutto, thinly
 sliced and chopped
4 scallions, diced
 Salt, to taste
½ teaspoon freshly ground
 black pepper
6 sprigs parsley, finely chopped
1 pound fresh peas, shelled

In a skillet, simmer the butter, prosciutto, scallions, salt, pepper, and parsley for 5 minutes. Add the peas and cook slowly for 2 or 3 minutes.

Serves 4.

Broccoli with Parmesan

1 large bunch broccoli
 Salt
 Pepper
2 cloves garlic, minced
3 tablespoons oil
3 tablespoons freshly grated
 Parmesan cheese
 Lemon wedges

Wash the broccoli, peel the stems, and trim the tough ends. Cut the broccoli into pieces and cook in boiling, salted water until just tender, about 10 to 12 minutes; drain. Sprinkle with the salt, pepper, garlic, oil, and cheese; toss gently. Serve with lemon wedges.

Serves 4 to 6.

Acorn Squash

2 acorn squash
4 tablespoons brown sugar
4 tablespoons butter

Preheat the oven to 375 degrees.

Remove the stems if still intact and cut each squash in half; remove and discard the seeds. Spread 1 tablespoon butter and sprinkle 1 tablespoon brown sugar in each half. Place the squash, cut sides up, in a baking pan. Pour water to a ¾-inch depth around the squash and bake until tender, about 1 hour.

Serves 4.

Asparagus with Lemon and Oil

1 pound asparagus
 Salt, to taste
¼ teaspoon freshly ground
 black pepper
2 cloves garlic, minced
4 tablespoons oil
 Juice of 1 lemon
¼ cup freshly grated Parmesan
 cheese

Snap off and discard the tough ends of the asparagus. Wash the asparagus thoroughly. Cook in 1 inch of simmering, salted water for 10 to 12 minutes; drain. Season with the salt, pepper, and garlic. Drizzle the oil and lemon juice over the asparagus. Sprinkle with grated cheese.

Serves 4.

Escarole with Skroodles

1½ to 2 pounds escarole
3 tablespoons vegetable oil
3 tablespoons butter
½ teaspoon freshly ground black pepper
1 teaspoon salt
¼ teaspoon dried oregano
1 pound skroodles or other curly noodles, cooked according to package directions until al dente and drained
¼ cup freshly grated Romano cheese

Clean the escarole. Cook the escarole in boiling water until tender, about 10 minutes; drain. Heat the oil and butter in a large saucepan. Add the escarole and seasonings. Gently toss in the skroodles. Sprinkle grated cheese on each serving.

Serves 4 to 6.

Ricotta Balls Florentine

1 pound fresh spinach or 10 ounces frozen spinach, cooked, squeezed dry, and finely chopped
1 pound ricotta cheese
1 teaspoon salt
¼ teaspoon freshly ground black pepper
1 teaspoon minced garlic
2 eggs
½ cup all-purpose flour
4 tablespoons butter, melted and still hot
¼ cup freshly grated Romano cheese

Bring a pot of water to a boil. Meanwhile, combine the spinach, ricotta, salt, pepper, garlic, and eggs. Shape the mixture into balls, about the size of golf balls; roll them in flour and drop them into the boiling water. Simmer for 4 to 5 minutes; they will float to the top when they are done. Remove the balls with a slotted spoon. Dip them first in the hot butter and then roll them in the Romano cheese. Serve immediately.

Serves 4.

Spinach al Romano

- 1 pound fresh spinach
- ½ cup water
- ¼ cup vegetable oil
- 1 teaspoon salt
- ¼ teaspoon freshly ground black pepper
- ¼ teaspoon freshly ground nutmeg
- ½ teaspoon minced garlic
- ¼ cup freshly grated Romano cheese

Clean the spinach thoroughly. Pour the water in a large saucepan. Add the spinach and cook it over moderate heat for 10 minutes. Add the oil, salt, pepper, nutmeg, and garlic. Simmer until thoroughly heated, about 3 to 4 minutes. Sprinkle with the cheese.

Serves 4.

Stuffed Eggplant

- 2 medium eggplants, unpeeled
- ½ cup vegetable oil
- 2 medium onions, chopped
- 2 cloves garlic, minced
- 1 teaspoon salt
- ¼ teaspoon freshly ground black pepper
- ¼ teaspoon dried oregano
- 4 tablespoons chopped fresh parsley
- 2 slices bread, soaked in water and squeezed dry
- ½ cup freshly grated Romano cheese
- 2 eggs
- Water
- 1½ cups Tomato Sauce (see page 79)

Preheat the oven to 375 degrees.

Cut each eggplant in half lengthwise. Scoop out the pulp, reserving the shells. Cube the eggplant pulp. Heat the oil in a large saucepan; sauté the eggplant, onions, garlic, salt, pepper, oregano, and parsley until the eggplant is soft. Pour the mixture into a large bowl. Combine the bread, cheese, and eggs with the eggplant mixture. Mix well. Fill the eggplant shells. Put the filled shells in a greased baking pan to which ¼ inch of water has been added. Pour the Tomato Sauce over each eggplant. Cover the pan with aluminum foil and bake for 1 hour.

Serves 4.

Broccoli Roll-Ups

1 to 1 ½ pounds broccoli
3 tablespoons all-purpose flour
1½ cups milk
2 tablespoons butter, melted
3 thin slices ham
½ cup freshly grated Romano cheese

Preheat the oven to 375 degrees.

Clean the broccoli thoroughly. Remove the hard stems, break into spears, and peel the skin to the florets. Bring 2 quarts of water to a rolling boil, add the broccoli, and cook it for 7 minutes; drain. Combine the flour and milk and slowly add the mixture to the melted butter. Roll each ham slice around some florets and place in a shallow, buttered casserole. Pour the milk-butter mixture over the roll-ups, sprinkle them with Romano cheese, and bake for 10 minutes.

Serves 4.

If you're cooking with canned tomatoes, use Italian plum tomatoes; American tomatoes are packed with too much water and are more discolored. Use fresh tomatoes if they are available.

Stuffed Tomatoes

8 anchovy fillets, cut into small pieces
2 teaspoons capers
1½ cups bread crumbs
½ cup freshly grated Romano cheese
1 teaspoon salt
¼ teaspoon freshly ground black pepper
2 cloves garlic, minced
4 tablespoons vegetable oil
8 firm tomatoes

Preheat the oven to 350 degrees.

Place the anchovies, capers, 1 cup of the bread crumbs, cheese, salt, pepper, and garlic in a blender or food processor and mix lightly. Add 1 tablespoon of the oil and blend. Cut the tomatoes in half crosswise and scoop out the pulp. Fill the tomato shells with the bread-crumb mixture. Sprinkle the remaining bread crumbs and drizzle the remaining oil over the filled tomatoes. Place the tomatoes in a greased baking dish and bake for 30 minutes.

Serves 8.

Celery Fritters

5 stalks celery, with leaves
1 cup all-purpose flour
2 eggs, beaten
  Salt
  Freshly ground black pepper
1 clove garlic, minced
¼ cup water
¼ cup freshly grated Parmesan
  cheese
1 cup oil

Wash the celery and chop it into ½-inch pieces. Combine the celery with the flour, eggs, salt, pepper, garlic, water, and cheese; mix well. (The mixture should have the consistency of pancake batter.)

Heat the oil in a skillet. When the oil is hot, drop the batter by tablespoonfuls into the oil and fry until golden brown on all sides. Drain on paper towels.

Serves 4 to 6.

Baked Celery Casserole

1 bunch celery
2 small onions
2 cloves garlic
1¼ cup Tomato Sauce (see
  page 79)
1 teaspoon salt
½ teaspoon freshly ground
  black pepper
½ cup freshly grated
  Parmesan or Romano
  cheese

Preheat the oven to 350 degrees. Bring a pot of water to a boil.

Cut the celery, including the leaves, into 3-inch pieces. Place the celery in the boiling water with the onions and garlic. Cook for 10 minutes; drain. Place a little Tomato Sauce on the bottom of a casserole. Put some of the celery mixture over the sauce and season with salt and pepper. Sprinkle with some of the cheese. Repeat the layers until you use all the ingredients. Bake, covered, for 15 to 20 minutes.

Serves 4.

Eggs & Rice

Eggs alla Anchovy

6 hard-boiled eggs
1 2-ounce can anchovy fillets
½ teaspoon prepared mustard
¼ teaspoon freshly ground
   black pepper
¼ teaspoon salt
½ teaspoon minced garlic
¼ teaspoon vinegar
1 tablespoon minced parsley
½ teaspoon olive oil
   Lettuce leaves

Peel the eggs, cut them in half lengthwise, and remove the yolks. Put the yolks in a small mixing bowl and add all the remaining ingredients except the lettuce. Mash and blend thoroughly. Spoon the mixture into the egg halves. Serve on a bed of lettuce leaves.

Serves 4 to 6.

Spinach and Eggs

¼ cup vegetable oil
1 pound fresh spinach, cleaned
   and cooked
1 teaspoon salt
¼ teaspoon freshly ground
   black pepper
1 clove garlic, minced
½ cup freshly grated Romano
   cheese
6 eggs, lightly beaten

Heat the oil in a large saucepan. Add the spinach, salt, pepper, garlic, and cheese. Mix well. Add the eggs. Cook, stirring, until the eggs are set.

Serves 4.

Small Ricotta Omelets

3 tablespoons all-purpose flour
3 tablespoons water
4 eggs
2 cups ricotta cheese
¼ teaspoon salt
¼ teaspoon freshly ground
   black pepper
¼ teaspoon dried oregano
1 teaspoon minced garlic
¼ cup freshly grated Romano
   cheese
   Vegetable oil or butter

Mix the flour with the water; beat in the eggs. In another bowl, use a fork to mix the ricotta thoroughly with the salt, pepper, oregano, garlic, and Romano cheese. Brush a nonstick griddle with the oil or butter. Place 2 tablespoons of the egg mixture on the griddle; cook slowly until the egg is set. Place 2 tablespoons of the ricotta mixture over the cooked egg and cover with another 2 tablespoons of egg mixture. Flip to cook the top for a moment. Keep the omelet warm on a heated plate. Make 3 more omelets in the same manner.

Serves 4.

Spaghetti and Sausage Omelet

....

¼ cup oil
1 small pepper, finely chopped
1 onion, finely chopped
1 clove garlic, minced
¼ pound Italian sausage, cooked and cut into small pieces
3 slices mozzarella cheese, cut into bits
8 eggs thoroughly beaten with ¼ cup milk
¼ cup freshly grated Romano cheese
½ pound spaghetti, cooked and drained

In an 8-inch nonstick skillet place the oil, pepper, onion, and garlic; sauté until the onions are transparent. Add the sausage, mozzarella, and beaten eggs. Sprinkle the omelet with the Romano cheese; add the spaghetti and mix well. Let the bottom of the omelet cook until set, then invert a plate over the frying pan and flip the omelet onto the plate. Slide the omelette back into the pan so that the uncooked side is down and cook until firm.

Serves 4.

Peas with Eggs

....

½ pound bacon, cut into small pieces
1 tablespoon butter
1 onion, finely chopped
2 cloves garlic, minced
1 teaspoon dried basil
1 teaspoon salt
¼ teaspoon freshly ground black pepper
1 pound shelled fresh or thawed frozen peas
3 eggs, well beaten
¼ cup freshly grated Romano cheese

Place the bacon and butter in a skillet and sauté until the bacon is lightly browned. Add the onion, garlic, basil, salt, and pepper; sauté until the onions are soft. Add the peas and cook for 2 to 3 minutes. Finally, add the eggs and stir for 2 to 3 minutes, cooking to desired texture. Sprinkle the cheese over all.

Serves 4 to 6.

Piedmont-Style Rice

2 small onions, minced
4 tablespoons butter
¼ pound prosciutto or chicken giblets, finely chopped
½ cup sliced mushrooms
2 cups uncooked rice
2 quarts hot beef or chicken broth (see page 40)
Pinch of salt
½ teaspoon freshly ground black pepper
½ teaspoon freshly ground nutmeg
½ cup freshly grated Parmesan cheese

Sauté the onions in the butter over medium heat until the onions are lightly browned. Add the prosciutto, mushrooms, 1 cup of the rice, and about 1 quart of the stock. Continue to stir while adding the remaining rice and stock. Cook until the rice is tender, about 12 to 15 minutes. (The rice should be moist but not too wet.) Season with the salt, pepper, and nutmeg. Sprinkle with the cheese.

Serves 6 to 8.

Italian Fried Rice with Bacon

2 cups uncooked rice
1 tablespoon vegetable oil
2 tablespoons butter
6 slices bacon, cut into pieces
2 medium onions, minced
½ cup freshly grated Romano cheese
1 teaspoon salt
¼ teaspoon freshly ground black pepper
½ teaspoon minced garlic
2 eggs

Cook the rice in a large quantity of boiling, salted water for 12 minutes; drain. Heat the oil and butter in a large skillet. Add the bacon and fry until crisp. Add the onions and sauté until they are transparent. Add the rice, cheese, salt, pepper, and garlic. Mix thoroughly. Add the eggs, one at a time, stirring after each addition. Cook until the eggs have set. Simmer, covered, over low heat for 5 minutes.

Serves 4.

Rice Balls

2 cups cooked rice
3 eggs, beaten
¼ cup all-purpose flour
1 cup freshly grated Romano
  cheese
  Salt, to taste
1 teaspoon freshly ground
  black pepper
3 cloves garlic, minced
2 sprigs parsley, chopped
1 cup bread crumbs
  Oil for frying

Mix together the rice, eggs, flour, ½ cup of the cheese, salt, pepper, garlic, and parsley. Taste for seasoning. Combine the bread crumbs and remaining cheese. Shape the rice mixture into small balls, about 1¼ inches in diameter. Dip the balls in the bread-crumb mixture. Heat about 1½ inches of oil in an 8- or 10-inch skillet. Fry the rice balls until they are golden brown on all sides.

Serves 6 to 8.

NOTE: This may be served as a side dish or as a hot hors d'oeuvre.

Venetian Risotto

¼ cup butter
2 chicken gizzards, cut into
  pieces
2 chicken livers, cut into pieces
2 cloves garlic, minced
1 small onion, chopped
1 6-ounce can tomato paste
12 ounces water (using the
   tomato paste can as a
   measure)
   Pinch of salt
¼ teaspoon freshly ground
  black pepper
½ teaspoon cinnamon
6 cups Chicken Broth (see
  page 40)
2 cups uncooked rice
½ cup freshly grated Parmesan
  cheese

Heat the butter in a saucepan. Add all the ingredients except the broth, rice, and cheese. Simmer slowly for 45 minutes. Bring the broth to a boil in a large pot. Stir in the simmered mixture and the rice, a little at a time, until all the ingredients are combined. Cook until the rice is tender, about 12 to 15 minutes. Stir in the cheese. Serve immediately.

Serves 6 to 8.

Milanese Risotto

6 cups Chicken Broth (see page 40)
⅛ teaspoon saffron threads
2 onions, chopped
9 tablespoons butter
2 cups uncooked rice
⅔ cup dry white wine
½ cup freshly grated Parmesan cheese

Bring the chicken broth to a boil in a 4-quart saucepan. Sprinkle in the saffron. In a heavy casserole, sauté the onions in 5 tablespoons of the butter until the onions are very lightly browned. Add the rice to the onions and cook, stirring, until the grains are coated with butter. Pour in the wine. Cook, stirring, for 5 minutes. Add the stock, a little at a time, stirring almost constantly. When all the stock has been added and the rice is soft, stir in the remaining 4 tablespoons of butter and the cheese. Serve piping hot.

Serves 4 to 6.

Chicken Liver Risotto Veneziana

¼ pound chicken livers, halved
2 medium onions, chopped
3 cloves garlic, minced
2 cups sliced mushrooms
3 tablespoons vegetable oil
3 tablespoons butter
¼ cup white wine
1 teaspoon salt
¼ teaspoon freshly ground black pepper
¼ teaspoon dried sage
4 cups Chicken Broth (see page 40)
2 cups uncooked rice
¼ cup freshly grated Romano cheese
2 tablespoons parsley

Sauté the chicken livers, onions, garlic, and mushrooms in the oil and butter until the livers are tender. Add the wine and season with the salt, pepper, and sage. Meanwhile, bring the chicken broth to a boil in a saucepan. Add the rice, reduce the heat, and simmer, covered, until the rice is tender, about 15 minutes. Add the cheese and parsley. Serve the chicken livers over the rice.

Serves 6.

Ham Frittata

¼ cup vegetable oil
2 medium onions, chopped
1 green pepper, minced
2 cloves garlic, minced
8 slices ham, diced
8 mushrooms, thinly sliced
8 eggs
1 teaspoon salt
¼ teaspoon freshly ground
  black pepper
¼ cup freshly grated Parmesan
  cheese

Preheat the oven to 375 degrees.

Heat the oil in a large skillet. Add the onions, green pepper, garlic, ham, and mushrooms; sauté until the onions are transparent. Thoroughly beat together the eggs, salt, and pepper in a bowl. Add the sautéed ingredients and the cheese; mix with a few strokes. Pour the mixture into a greased square or oblong pan and bake until a knife inserted in the center comes out clean, about 45 minutes.

Serves 4 to 6.

Artichoke Frittata

1 10-ounce package frozen
  artichoke hearts, thawed
1 tablespoon lemon juice
2 tablespoons vegetable oil
2 tablespoons butter
1 cup all-purpose flour
6 eggs
3 tablespoons water
1 teaspoon salt
¼ teaspoon freshly ground
  black pepper
½ teaspoon minced garlic
½ cup freshly grated Romano
  cheese

Preheat the oven to 350 degrees.

Cut the artichoke hearts in half lengthwise. Sprinkle with the lemon juice. Heat the oil and butter in a large skillet. Dredge the artichoke hearts in the flour and brown them on each side until golden. Remove the artichoke hearts to a greased 2-quart casserole.

Beat the eggs and water together until blended. Combine the salt, pepper, garlic, and cheese; add them to the eggs and mix well. Pour the eggs over the artichoke hearts and bake until a knife inserted in the center of the casserole comes out clean, 20 to 25 minutes.

Serves 4.

Eggs Florentine

¼ cup plus 2 tablespoons
   vegetable oil
 1 pound fresh spinach,
   washed, dried, and torn
   into pieces
1½ teaspoons salt
 ¼ teaspoon freshly ground
   black pepper
 ¼ cup freshly grated Romano
   cheese
 4 eggs

Preheat the oven to 350 degrees.

Heat ¼ cup of the oil in a large saucepan.
Add the spinach. Cook, covered, until tender,
about 10 minutes. Mix in the salt, pepper, and
cheese. Divide the spinach mixture among
four individual baking dishes. Break one egg
into each. Drizzle each with some of the remaining oil. Bake until the eggs are set, about
10 minutes.

Serves 4.

I've seen people throw the green part
of scallions away. Chop the tops. Put
them in olive oil and brown them a
little. Then add eggs to them and see
how they taste. Delicious!

Sam's Omelet Italiano

 ¼ cup oil
 5 potatoes, peeled and thinly
   sliced
 2 cups sliced mushrooms
 1 cup diced green peppers
 1 onion, chopped
 4 cloves garlic, minced
 1 teaspoon salt
 1 teaspoon freshly ground
   black pepper
 ¼ cup freshly grated Romano
   cheese
 6 eggs, well beaten

Heat the oil in a large skillet; sauté the
potatoes until almost soft, about 15 minutes.
Add the mushrooms, green peppers, onion,
and garlic; cook until the onions are soft.
Thoroughly mix in the salt and pepper. Add
the cheese and eggs and cook, stirring, over
medium heat. When the bottom of the omelet
is set, invert a plate over the skillet, turn out
the omelet onto the plate, and then slide the
omelet back into the skillet so that the uncooked side of the omelet is down. Cook until
set, about 5 more minutes. Serve hot.

Serves 4.

Breads

Basic Bread

1 ¼-ounce package active dry yeast
1 cup warm water (105 to 110 degrees)
4 cups all-purpose flour
1 teaspoon salt
1 teaspoon sugar
3 eggs, beaten
⅓ cup oil

Dissolve the yeast in the warm water. Mix the flour, salt, and sugar in a large bowl. Add the eggs. Make a well in the center of the flour and pour in the oil. Add the yeast and water and mix well. Keep adding more warm water, ¼ cup at a time, until most of the flour has been moistened by the liquid.

Knead the dough until it is elastic. If the dough is too sticky, add a little more flour; if it's too dry, add a little more water. (The dough has been properly kneaded when an indentation made with your finger springs back.) Cover the dough with a towel and let it rise in a warm place until doubled in bulk.

Divide the dough in half; shape each half into either a square loaf to be baked in a greased bread pan or into a round loaf to be baked on a greased cookie sheet. Let each rise until double again.

Preheat the oven to 375 degrees. Bake for 45 minutes to 1 hour.

Makes 2 loaves.

NOTE: This same recipe can be used as pizza dough or for Italian Doughnuts (see page 144).

Sautéed Garlic Bread

Butter
8 slices day-old bread
1 tablespoon minced garlic
¼ cup freshly grated Parmesan cheese

Butter each slice of bread on both sides. In a heavy skillet cook the bread on both sides until golden brown. Sprinkle one side of each slice with garlic and cheese. Serve hot.

Garlic Bread with Romano

1 loaf French bread
Butter as needed
3 cloves garlic, mashed
½ cup freshly grated Romano cheese

Preheat the oven to 325 degrees.

Cut the bread into ½-inch-thick slices, but do not cut all the way through the bottom crust. Generously butter the cut sides of the bread and sprinkle each slice with a little of the mashed garlic and some cheese. Put the loaf into a brown paper bag and bake for about 15 to 20 minutes. Serve warm.

Serves 4 to 6.

Garlic Bread

6 tablespoons butter, at room temperature
Salt and freshly ground black pepper, to taste
2 garlic cloves, mashed
1 loaf French bread, cut lengthwise
2 to 3 thin slices mozzarella cheese

Preheat the broiler.

Mash the butter with the salt, pepper, and garlic. Spread the mixture on the cut sides of the bread and cover each side with mozzarella cheese. Broil until the cheese is melted.

Serves 4 to 6.

John's Sausage Bread

1 cup milk
8 tablespoons butter
⅓ cup sugar
½ teaspoon salt
2 ¼-ounce packages active dry yeast
¼ cup warm water (105 to 110 degrees)
3 eggs
6 to 7 cups all-purpose flour

Filling

2 pounds coarsely ground pork butt
1 cup chopped green bell pepper
1 cup chopped onion
1 ½ teaspoons salt
¼ teaspoon freshly ground black pepper
1 ½ teaspoons fennel seeds
1 tablespoon fresh basil
1 egg beaten with 2 tablespoons water
1 tablespoon poppy seeds

Scald the milk and pour it over the butter, sugar, and salt in a large mixing bowl; blend and cool. Sprinkle the yeast over the warm water. Let the yeast stand for a few minutes then stir until dissolved. Stir the yeast and water into the cooled milk mixture. Add the eggs and 3 cups of the flour; beat until smooth. Stir in enough of the remaining flour to make a stiff dough. Turn the dough out onto a lightly floured board. Knead the dough well, put it in a greased bowl, cover, and let it stand at room temperature until doubled in bulk.

While waiting for the dough to rise, make the filling. In a large skillet, cook the pork, green pepper, and onion over low heat, stirring often, until the meat is crumbly. About halfway through the cooking time, add the salt, pepper, fennel seeds, and basil. When the meat is completely cooked, drain off and discard the excess liquid; set the meat mixture aside.

When the dough has doubled in size, punch it down and let it rest for a few minutes. Preheat the oven to 375 degrees.

On a lightly floured board, roll the dough into a circle about 12 inches in diameter. Spread the meat mixture over the entire surface, leaving a margin of about 1 inch all around. Roll the dough up like a jelly roll, bend it to form a circle, and pinch the ends together. Place the roll on a large, greased baking pan. Brush it with the egg wash and sprinkle it with poppy seeds.

Bake for about 45 minutes. Cool and slice.

Makes 1 loaf.

Easter Bread Loaves
....

      2 ¼-ounce packages active
         dry yeast
    ½ cup warm water (105 to
         110 degrees)
      8 tablespoons butter, softened
      2 cups warm milk
      8 cups all-purpose flour
      3 eggs
1 ¼ cups sugar
      1 teaspoon salt
         Grated rind of 1 lemon
      1 cup chopped walnuts
1 ½ cups raisins
    ½ teaspoon cinnamon
      6 hard-boiled eggs, peeled
         Frosting (recipe follows)

Preheat the oven to 375 degrees.

Dissolve the yeast in the warm water. Add the softened butter, milk, flour, eggs, sugar, salt, lemon rind, walnuts, raisins, and cinnamon; combine thoroughly. Turn the dough out onto a lightly floured surface and knead until smooth and elastic. Form the dough into 3 loaves, reserving a little dough. Place 2 eggs on each loaf. Make small strips with the reserved dough and crisscross the strips over the eggs so they stay in place. Let the loaves rise until doubled in bulk. Bake on greased cookie sheets for 45 minutes. Let them cool before spreading with the frosting.

Makes 3 loaves.

Frosting

      2 cups confectioners' sugar
    ½ cup warm water

Mix the confectioners' sugar and warm water.

Nut Muffins
....

      1 cup all-purpose flour
      1 cup whole wheat flour
      1 teaspoon baking powder
    ⅔ cup sugar
      1 teaspoon salt
    ½ cup chopped walnuts
      4 tablespoons vegetable
         shortening
      2 eggs
      1 cup milk

Preheat the oven to 375 degrees.

Sift the two flours together. Add the baking powder, sugar, salt, and walnuts. Cut the shortening into the dry ingredients; mix thoroughly. Beat the eggs and milk together and add to the other ingredients. Grease or use paper muffin cups in tins and fill them ⅔ full with batter. Bake until a toothpick inserted into the center muffin comes out clean, about 30 minutes.

Makes 15 to 20 muffins.

Desserts

Mama D's Cookies

5 eggs
2 cups sugar
1 cup vegetable oil
1 cup golden raisins, soaked in warm water and drained
½ cup milk
½ teaspoon salt
¼ teaspoon freshly ground black pepper
1 teaspoon cinnamon
½ teaspoon ground allspice
5 to 6 cups all-purpose flour
1 teaspoon baking powder
1 teaspoon baking soda
⅔ cup finely chopped walnuts

Preheat the oven to 375 degrees.

Beat the eggs in a bowl. Beat in the sugar, oil, raisins, milk, salt, pepper, cinnamon, and allspice. Combine the flour, baking powder, and baking soda and add to the egg mixture; mix well. Shape the dough into small balls; roll the balls in the walnuts and place 1 inch apart on a greased cookie sheet. Bake about 15 minutes.

Makes about 4 dozen cookies.

Almond Cookies

3 eggs
1 cup sugar
Juice and grated rind of 1 lemon, prepared separately
1 teaspoon vanilla extract
½ cup milk
4 cups all-purpose flour
3 teaspoons baking powder
½ cup shortening
½ cup chopped almonds

Preheat the oven to 325 degrees.

Cream the eggs and sugar together. Add the lemon juice, vanilla, and ¼ cup of the milk. In another bowl, mix the flour and baking powder together and cut in the shortening. Stir the almonds and grated lemon rind into the flour-shortening mixture; alternately add this and the remaining ¼ cup milk to the egg mixture, blending well. Make 3 or 4 long, 2-inch-thick rolls. Place the rolls on a greased cookie sheet and bake for 25 to 30 minutes. Remove the rolls from the cookie sheet and, while still warm, cut them at an angle into ½-inch-thick slices.

Makes 5 to 6 dozen cookies.

Cannoli

2 ½ cups all-purpose flour
2 eggs, beaten
2 tablespoons vegetable oil
1 teaspoon sugar
Pinch of salt
1 cup wine vinegar
¼ cup water
1 egg, beaten with 1
tablespoon water
Vegetable oil for frying

Filling

1 ½ pounds ricotta cheese
1 ½ cups sugar
1 tablespoon cinnamon
1 teaspoon vanilla extract
Chocolate sprinkles
Confectioners' sugar

Thoroughly mix the flour, eggs, oil, sugar, salt, and wine vinegar. Slowly add the water. Knead the dough on a floured surface until you can form the dough into a ball. With your hands, make a roll 1 inch in diameter; cut it into ¼-inch-thick slices. Roll each slice into an oval about the thickness of pie dough. Fold the longer sides of each oval around a cannoli tube ¾ inch in diameter and 5 to 6 inches in length. Press the longer edges together and seal with the egg wash.

Heat the oil in a deep, heavy pan. Fry the cannoli shells until a golden brown. Cool.

Mix the filling ingredients together, except for the sprinkles and the sugar. Just before serving, stuff each cannoli shell with some of the filling, decorate the edges with chocolate sprinkles, and sprinkle confectioners' sugar over all.

Makes 3 dozen cannoli.

Coffee Bread Pudding

2 cups dry bread cubes
1 ½ cups hot milk
3 eggs, beaten
1 ½ cups strong coffee
¾ cup sugar
¼ teaspoon salt
3 tablespoons butter, at room temperature
1 ½ teaspoons vanilla extract
½ cup chopped nuts
Whipped cream, optional

Preheat the oven to 375 degrees.

Thoroughly combine the bread, milk, eggs, coffee, sugar, salt, and butter. Add the vanilla and nuts and mix again. Pour the mixture into a greased 8-by-8-by-2-inch baking dish. Bake until firm, about 40 minutes. Serve the pudding either hot or cold and with a dollop of whipped cream on top if you like.

Serves 6.

Dinkytown Two-Egg Cake

¾ cup sugar
½ cup shortening
2 eggs, beaten
1 teaspoon vanilla extract
2 cups all-purpose flour, sifted
2 teaspoons baking powder
½ teaspoon salt
⅔ cup milk
    Confectioners' sugar

Preheat the oven to 375 degrees.

Thoroughly cream the sugar and shortening in a bowl. Stir in the eggs and vanilla. Sift together the flour, baking powder, and salt. Alternately add the dry ingredients and the milk to the egg-sugar mixture. Beat thoroughly after each addition until smooth. Pour the batter into a greased 8-by-8-by-2-inch cake pan. Bake until the cake springs back when indented gently with a finger, about 25 minutes. Let the cake cool. Sprinkle the top of the cake with confectioners' sugar.

Serves 10 to 12.

Jelly Turnovers

2 ½ cups all-purpose flour
¼ cup sugar
½ cup white wine
½ teaspoon salt
2 tablespoons oil
    Turnover Filling
    Oil for frying
    Confectioners' sugar

Mix the flour, sugar, wine, salt, and 2 tablespoons of oil. Roll the dough out as if for a pie. Cut the dough into 3-by-3-inch squares. Put 2 tablespoons of filling on each square. For each turnover, fold one corner over to its opposite corner and seal the edges with a fork. Deep-fry the turnovers in hot oil until golden brown on both sides. Sprinkle with the confectioners' sugar.

Makes about 30 turnovers.

Turnover Filling

½ cup orange marmalade
¼ cup raisins
½ cup peach preserves
½ teaspoon cinnamon
¼ cup finely chopped walnuts

Blend all the ingredients together.

Easter Panettone

....

    2 ¼-ounce packages active
      dry yeast
    ½ cup warm water (105 to
      110 degrees)
    6 cups all-purpose flour
    ⅔ cups sugar
    1 teaspoon salt
    1 cup vegetable oil
    1 cup chopped citron or
      dried fruits
    ⅔ cup raisins
    ½ cup walnuts or almonds
    1½ teaspoons anise seeds
    4 eggs
    ½ cup milk
    ½ cup water
      Frosting
      Walnuts or almonds, for
      garnish

Dissolve the yeast in the warm water. In a bowl, thoroughly mix the flour, sugar, salt, oil, citron, raisins, walnuts, and anise seeds. Blend in the dissolved yeast, eggs, milk, and water. On a floured surface, knead the dough, adding more flour or water as needed to make a soft dough. Cover and let it rise until doubled in bulk. Cut the dough into 6 pieces. Place one piece of dough in each of 6 well-greased, clean coffee cans; let the dough rise again for 30 minutes.

Preheat the oven to 350 degrees. Bake for about 40 minutes; allow the panettone to cool in the cans.

Remove the panettone from the cans and frost the tops and sides. Decorate them with walnuts or almonds on top.

Makes 6 loaves.

Frosting

    1 cup confectioners' sugar
      Warm water

Mix the confectioners' sugar with enough warm water to make a frosting of spreadable consistency.

> Hands are the best mixers in the world. They beat any electric mixer.

Mama D's Cheesecake

3 cups ricotta cheese
1 cup sugar
Grated rind of 1 orange
Grated rind of 1 lemon
1 tablespoon vanilla extract
4 eggs, beaten
½ cup all-purpose flour
1 8-ounce carton sour cream
¼ cup sugar

Preheat the oven to 375 degrees.

Mix together the cheese, 1 cup of sugar, the orange and lemon rinds, vanilla, and eggs; blend until smooth. Add the flour and mix again. Pour the batter into a greased 8-by-8-inch baking dish and bake for 70 minutes.

Mix the sour cream and ¼ cup of sugar together and spread over the cheesecake for a topping. Bake the cake for 10 minutes more.

Cool and serve.

Serves 6 to 8.

Gelati (Ice Cream) alla Ruma

3 eggs, separated
4 tablespoons sugar
2 cups whipped cream
1 teaspoon vanilla extract
4 tablespoons rum

In a bowl, beat the egg whites until stiff. In another bowl, beat the sugar and egg yolks until frothy and thick. Fold in the egg whites and whipped cream. Stir in the vanilla and rum. Pour the mixture into a quart container and freeze until solid, about 3 hours.

Serves 4.

Lemon Ice

2 cups water
1 cup sugar
1 cup lemon juice

In a 2-quart saucepan, bring the water and sugar to a boil, stirring until the sugar dissolves. Boil the mixture for 5 minutes more. Remove the pan from the heat; cool. Stir in the lemon juice. Pour the mixture into a freezer tray and freeze, stirring occasionally, until the mixture is the texture of snow, about 4 hours. Serve in tall, slender stemmed glasses.

Serves 4.

Blueberry Spumoni

1 quart blueberries, washed
   and drained
2 teaspoons lemon juice
¼ cup sugar
1 pint heavy cream
⅔ cup confectioners' sugar

Crush the blueberries. Add the lemon juice and sugar to the berries. Whip the cream until it stands in soft peaks; fold in the confectioners' sugar. Combine the cream with the blueberries. Place the mixture in a 1-quart mold or 8 stemmed glasses and freeze for at least 2 hours.

Serves 8.

Zeppoli

1 cup hot water
8 tablespoons butter
2 tablespoons sugar
½ teaspoon salt
2½ cups all-purpose flour
4 eggs
   Grated rind of 1 lemon
   Grated rind of 1 orange

Preheat the oven to 400 degrees.

In a saucepan, bring the water, butter, sugar, and salt to a boil. Add the flour all at once, beating with a wooden spoon. Remove the pan from the heat. Add 1 egg at a time, beating well after each addition. (The dough should be smooth and glossy.) Stir in the grated rinds.

Drop the dough by tablespoonfuls 2½ inches apart onto a greased cookie sheet. Bake for 10 minutes. Lower the oven temperature to 350 degrees and bake until golden, about 15 minutes more. Cool the zeppoli on a wire rack.

Makes 1 dozen zeppoli.

Pizzelle Cookies

1½ cups sugar
16 tablespoons margarine or
   butter
3 teaspoons anise seeds
6 eggs
1 teaspoon salt
½ cup milk
1 teaspoon vanilla extract
3½ cups all-purpose flour

Cream together the sugar and margarine. Add the anise, eggs, salt, milk, and vanilla. Add the flour gradually, forming a soft dough. Roll the dough into walnut-size balls. Heat a Pizzelle iron. For each cookie, place a dough ball in the center of the iron; close the iron and hold its handles tightly together for 1 to 1½ minutes.

Makes 3½ dozen cookies.

Caramel Pudding

1¾ cups sugar
1 quart milk
7 eggs
1 teaspoon salt
2 teaspoons vanilla extract

Preheat the oven to 325 degrees.

Caramelize 1 cup of the sugar in a heavy skillet over low heat. Pour the sugar into a warm mold, coating all sides. Scald the milk; cool slightly. Beat the eggs just until combined. Mix in the remaining sugar, the salt, and vanilla. Blend in the milk, a little at a time. Strain the mixture through a sieve into the coated mold. Place the mold in a pan of water that comes to half the height of the mold and bake until a knife inserted in the center comes out clean, about 1 to 1½ hours. Refrigerate the pudding for at least 1 hour before serving. Invert it on a serving plate to unmold.

Serves 6 to 8.

Mama D's Italian Fruit Cake

3½ cups all-purpose flour
½ cup vegetable oil
½ cup water
½ cup wine
2 tablespoons whiskey or brandy
¼ cup sugar
2 cups raisins
2 cups chopped walnuts
1 pound figs, chopped
Vegetable oil
Sugar

Preheat the oven to 375 degrees.

Put the flour in a large mixing bowl and make a well in the center. Combine the oil, water, wine, and whiskey; pour the mixture into the well in the flour and combine. On a floured surface, knead the dough until it is elastic. Combine the sugar, raisins, walnuts, and figs in another bowl.

On a floured surface, roll the dough out into 2 thin circles about 14 inches in diameter. Place half the raisin mixture over one dough circle, roll it up like a jelly roll, and bring the ends together to form a ring; pinch the ends together to seal. Repeat with the second circle. Brush the tops with oil and sprinkle with sugar. Bake on greased cookie sheets until the cakes are a light golden brown, about 45 minutes.

Makes 2 fruit cakes, serving 8 to 10 each.

Italian Doughnuts (Pizza Fritta)

1 recipe Basic Bread (see page 131)
Oil for frying
Sugar or honey for glaze

Prepare the Basic Bread dough. After the dough has risen the first time, fill a heavy skillet ⅔ full of oil. Heat the oil until a cube of bread dropped in the oil browns quickly. Form small pieces of dough into rounds; poke your thumb through the centers to make a hole in each. Drop the rounds, a few at a time, into the hot oil. Turn when the doughnuts are golden brown on one side. When the second side is golden, remove the doughnuts from the oil and drain them on paper towels. Sprinkle with sugar or drizzle with honey. Serve hot or cold.

Makes about 24 3-inch doughnuts.

Doughnuts for Christmas

2 ¼-ounce packages active dry yeast
2 cups warm water (105 to 110 degrees)
6 cups flour
¼ cup sugar
1½ teaspoons salt
¼ cup oil
3 eggs
Sugar
Oil for frying
Confectioners' sugar or cinnamon and sugar mixed together

Dissolve the yeast in the warm water. When bubbly, add the flour, sugar, salt, oil, and eggs. On a floured surface knead the dough thoroughly, adding more water or flour if necessary. Cover and let the dough rise until doubled in bulk. For each doughnut, form a small piece of dough into a ball about 2 inches in diameter; punch a hole in the center with your thumb. Place the doughnuts on a pan and let them rise. Heat 1 inch of oil in a heavy skillet and deep-fry the doughnuts until golden brown on both sides; drain on paper towels and sprinkle with one of the sugars.

Makes 18 doughnuts.

Crespele Doughnuts

1 cup warm milk
1 cup water (105 to 110 degrees)
1 ¼-ounce package active dry yeast
2½ cups flour
1 teaspoon salt
½ cup sugar mixed with 1 teaspoon cinnamon
¼ cup vegetable oil
Oil for frying
Cinnamon mixed with sugar, for topping

Combine the milk and water and dissolve the yeast in them. Mix the flour, salt, sugar mixture, and oil in a bowl. Stir in the yeast solution. On a floured surface, knead the dough until smooth and elastic. Let it rise until doubled in bulk. Roll the dough out until ¼-inch thick; cut the dough into either 2-inch rounds or 8-by-½-inch strips that you tie together in a loose knot. Heat 2 inches of vegetable oil in a deep skillet and fry the doughnuts until golden on all sides. Remove and drain them on paper towels. Sprinkle with sugar and cinnamon while hot.

Makes 2 to 3 dozen.

Rice Pudding

⅔ cup uncooked rice
2 cups cold water
3 cups milk
5 egg yolks
1 cup sugar
1 teaspoon salt
1 teaspoon cinnamon

In a saucepan, combine the rice, water, and milk; simmer until the rice is soft, about 15 minutes. Beat the egg yolks and sugar until thick. Gradually stir in the rice mixture, blend well, and return all of the egg-rice mixture to the saucepan. Add the salt and cook, stirring constantly, until thickened, about 2 more minutes. Divide the mixture among 6 pudding dishes; sprinkle each with cinnamon. Serve warm or chilled.

Serves 6.

If you want an extra clear pot of brewed coffee, try making it the Scandinavian way—with egg. Beat one egg and mix it with the ground coffee; throw it right into the coffeepot, and let it brew. Then let the coffee stand for a few minutes and strain before serving.

Ricotta Cheese Pudding

¼ cup white raisins
6 tablespoons mixed candied citrus rinds
¼ cup rum
2 tablespoons butter
Bread crumbs
4 eggs, separated
1 whole egg
1½ pounds ricotta cheese, put through a fine sieve
5 teaspoons all-purpose flour
6 tablespoons confectioners' sugar
½ teaspoon cinnamon

Preheat the oven to 375 degrees.

Soften the raisins and candied rinds in the rum for a few minutes. Butter a baking dish and coat it with bread crumbs. Beat the 4 egg yolks and 1 whole egg until combined. In another bowl, beat the 4 egg whites until stiff. Put the ricotta in a large bowl; add the yolk mixture, raisins, candied rinds, rum, flour, sugar, and cinnamon. If the mixture is not sweet enough, add more sugar. Fold in the egg whites. Fill an 8-by-10-by-2-inch baking dish half full. Bake the pudding for 1 hour. Serve it hot or cold.

Serves 4 to 6.

Stewed Apples with Cinnamon

4 to 6 cooking apples
1½ cups water
5 tablespoons sugar
2 tablespoons butter
1 teaspoon cinnamon

Peel the apples and cut them into ½-inch-thick wedges. Put the water in a saucepan and add the apples. Cook, covered, over low heat until the apples are tender, about 10 minutes. Add the sugar and simmer, uncovered, for 5 minutes. Mix in the butter and cinnamon; stir until the butter is melted. Cool and serve.

Serves 4.

Macaroons

4 egg whites
½ teaspoon salt
2 cups sugar
½ cup blanched almonds, finely ground
1 teaspoon almond extract

Preheat the oven to 350 degrees.

Beat the egg whites and salt until they are creamy. Add the sugar a little at a time; beat until peaks are stiff. Fold in the almonds and the almond extract. Drop the batter by tablespoonfuls ¾-inch apart onto cookie sheets lined with unglazed paper. Bake until light brown, about 10 to 12 minutes.

Makes about 5 dozen macaroons.

Mandole

4 eggs
1¼ cups sugar
½ cup oil
½ cup chopped almonds
   Juice and grated rind of 1 lemon
1½ teaspoons vanilla extract
½ teaspoon almond extract
3 teaspoons baking powder
3 cups all-purpose flour

Preheat the oven to 325 degrees.

Beat the eggs and sugar together until combined. Add the oil, almonds, lemon juice, grated rind, and vanilla and almond extracts. Mix the baking powder and flour together and add to the egg-sugar mixture. Knead the dough on a floured surface. Shape the dough into 10-inch-long, 2-inch-thick rolls. Place the rolls on greased and floured cookie sheets. Bake them until golden brown, about 25 minutes. Remove the rolls from the cookie sheets and, while still warm, cut them into ½-inch-thick slices.

Makes 6 to 8 dozen cookies.

Ricotta and Strawberry Crepes

2 tablespoons butter
½ cup sifted all-purpose flour
2 eggs plus 2 egg yolks, beaten
2 cups milk
5 tablespoons sugar
   Pinch of salt
⅔ pound ricotta cheese
1 teaspoon vanilla extract
1 pint strawberries, washed, hulled, and crushed
   Confectioners' sugar

Melt the butter. In a small bowl, mix together the flour, eggs plus yolks, milk, 1 tablespoon of the sugar, and the salt; blend well. Heat a 6-inch skillet or 6-inch crepe pan; brush it with the melted butter. For each crepe, pour in about 3 tablespoons of the batter, rotating the pan to spread the batter evenly. Cook the crepe on both sides. Stack the crepes as they are cooked; cover them with wax paper until you're ready to fill them.

Cream the ricotta with the remaining sugar and the vanilla. Add the strawberries and mix gently. Spoon some of the mixture into the center of each crepe and roll it up. Sprinkle with confectioners' sugar.

Serves 6.

Apple Fritters

¼ teaspoon salt
1½ cups all-purpose flour
3 tablespoons sugar
3 eggs, beaten
½ teaspoon cinnamon
1 cup milk or water
1 tablespoon melted butter or oil
3 apples, unpeeled and chopped or thinly sliced
Oil for frying
Cinnamon mixed with sugar

Mix the salt, flour, sugar, eggs, cinnamon, milk, and melted butter in a bowl. (The mixture should have the consistency of pancake batter; add a little more milk or flour if necessary.) Add the apples and mix well. Heat about 1 inch of oil in a skillet. Drop the batter by tablespoonfuls into the hot oil; brown on all sides. Drain the fritters on paper towels and sprinkle them with a mixture of cinnamon and sugar.

Makes about 18 fritters.

St. Joseph's Cakes

¼ cup sugar
3 eggs
¾ cup milk
3 cups all-purpose flour
Pinch of salt
3 teaspoons baking powder
Oil for frying
Confectioners' sugar

Beat together the sugar and eggs until light and fluffy. Stir in the milk. Mix the flour, salt, and baking powder together. Stir into the sugar-egg mixture and beat until smooth. Let the batter stand for 30 minutes.

Heat the oil to 375 degrees in a deep skillet. Drop the batter by tablespoonfuls into the oil and fry until golden brown on all sides. Remove each cake with a slotted spoon and drain on paper towels. Sprinkle the cakes with confectioners' sugar.

Serves 8 to 10.

Biscuit Tortoni

½ cup crushed toasted almonds
½ cup crushed macaroons
2 cups heavy cream
3 tablespoons dark rum
¼ cup confectioners' sugar
3 or 4 maraschino cherries, halved

Reserve 2 tablespoons of the almonds for the topping. Mix the remaining almonds, macaroons, and 1 cup of the cream. Whip the remaining cup of cream with the rum and sugar until soft peaks form. Fold the whipped cream into the almond-macaroon mixture. Spoon the mixture into 6 to 8 small dessert dishes and freeze it until it is firm, about 2 hours. Top each cup with a cherry half and a sprinkle of toasted almonds. Return the cups to the freezer until ready to serve.

Serves 6 to 8.

Sesame Cookies

3 cups all-purpose flour
1 cup sugar
2 teaspoons baking powder
Pinch of salt
1 cup shortening
3 eggs, beaten
¼ cup milk
1 cup sesame seeds

Preheat the oven to 375 degrees.

Mix the flour, sugar, baking powder, and salt; cut in the shortening. Add the eggs and milk; mix well. Pinch off pieces of the dough and form them into 1½-inch balls. Roll the balls in the sesame seeds. Place the cookies about ½-inch apart on a greased cookie sheet. Bake until light brown, about 20 minutes.

Makes 6 to 8 dozen cookies.

Don't throw out stale cake or cookies. Grind them up and mix them with cream frosting and use for a coffee cake filling. It makes the best coffee cake filling there is.

Spumoni

1 cup milk

½ cup sugar

¼ teaspoon salt

4 egg yolks, beaten

1 1-ounce square unsweetened chocolate

2 cups heavy cream

2 teaspoons rum extract

2 tablespoons sugar

⅛ teaspoon pistachio extract or ¼ cup chopped pistachio nuts

2 or 3 drops green food coloring

1 4-ounce jar maraschino cherries, drained, chopped, and chilled

6 almonds, finely chopped

½ teaspoon almond extract

Chill a bowl, rotary beaters, and a 1-quart mold.

Scald the milk in the top of a double boiler that is placed over, not in, boiling water. Stir in ½ cup sugar and the salt. Stir 3 tablespoons of the hot mixture into the egg yolks. Immediately pour the egg-milk mixture back into the top of the double boiler. Cook over simmering water until the mixture coats a spoon; remove from the heat and cool.

Melt the chocolate and set aside. Stir 1 cup of the heavy cream into the cooled custard mixture. Divide the mixture between 2 bowls. Add the melted chocolate to one bowl; mix well and refrigerate. Add the rum extract to the mixture in the second bowl; pour it into a freezer tray and freeze until mushy. Then remove the rum custard to a bowl and beat it with the chilled rotary beaters until smooth and creamy. Put it into the chilled mold and freeze until firm.

Beat ½ cup of the heavy cream until it stands in peaks. Add 1 tablespoon of the sugar and the pistachio extract. Fold in the green food coloring. Spoon the pistachio mixture over the frozen rum ice cream. Return the mold to the freezer. When the mixture is firm, spread the maraschino cherries on top. Return it to the freezer.

Beat the remaining ½ cup of the heavy cream in the chilled bowl with rotary beaters until it stands in peaks. Fold in the remaining tablespoon sugar, the almonds, and the almond extract. Spoon the almond mixture over the pistachio ice cream and maraschino cherries. Return it to the freezer.

When the almond ice cream is firm, pour the chocolate mixture into a freezer tray. Freeze it until mushy. Then put it into a chilled bowl and beat it with rotary beaters until creamy and smooth. Spoon the chocolate mixture over the almond ice cream.

Cover the mold with plastic wrap and freeze for 8 hours, or until firm. To unmold the ice cream, dip the mold into warm water for a few seconds and invert it on a serving plate.

Serves 6 to 8.

Almond Bread Pudding

3½ cups milk
8 tablespoons butter
2 cups dry stale bread, cut into cubes
¾ cup sugar
3 eggs, beaten
1 teaspoon vanilla extract
1 teaspoon cinnamon
1 teaspoon mace
1 cup raisins
1 cup chopped, blanched almonds

Preheat the oven to 375 degrees.

Scald the milk; add the butter to the milk, stirring until the butter is melted. Put the bread in a mixing bowl; pour the milk-butter mixture over the bread. Soak for 7 minutes. Add the remaining ingredients. (If the raisins are dry, soak them in warm water and drain them before adding.) Mix all together thoroughly. Pour the mixture into a buttered casserole or baking dish. Set the casserole in a pan of hot water that comes to half the height of the casserole. Bake until a knife inserted in the center of the pudding comes out clean, about 1 hour. Serve warm or cold.

Serves 6 to 8.

Italian Rum Cake

6 eggs, separated
½ cup sugar
1 tablespoon lemon juice
1 tablespoon orange juice
2 teaspoons rum extract
1 cup cake flour
Pinch of salt
Confectioners' sugar

Preheat the oven to 350 degrees.

Beat the egg yolks until thick. Beat in the sugar, lemon and orange juices, and rum extract. Sift the flour twice; gradually add the flour to the egg yolk mixture. Beat the egg whites until foamy; add the salt and beat until stiff. Fold the egg whites into the egg yolk mixture. Pour the batter into a greased 8-inch springform pan. Bake for 1 hour. Cool the cake in the pan. When the cake is completely cool, remove it from the pan and sprinkle it with confectioners' sugar.

Serves 4 to 6.

Try different brands of coffee until you find the blend you like. Select the grind for your kind of coffeepot. I still think the old enameled coffeepots make the best coffee. You really get the true coffee flavor when you put the coffee grounds right into the water. A good formula for coffee making that pleases most people is to add one heaping tablespoon of coffee for each cup and then one extra teaspoon for the pot.

St. Joseph's Day Sweet Ravioli

    2 cups ricotta cheese
      Sugar to taste
    1 teaspoon cinnamon
    2 eggs, beaten
      Ravioli Dough (see page 93)
      Oil for deep-frying
      Confectioners' sugar

Mix the ricotta, sugar, cinnamon, and eggs very thoroughly; set aside.

Follow the basic instructions for preparing Ravioli, but use the ricotta mixture for the filling. Deep-fry the filled ravioli in the hot oil until golden brown on both sides. Drain them on paper towels and sprinkle with confectioners' sugar.

Serves 6 to 8.

Honey Clusters

    2 cups sifted all-purpose flour
    1/4 teaspoon salt
    3 eggs
    1 teaspoon vanilla extract
      Oil for frying
    1/2 cup honey
    1/2 cup sugar
      Multicolored candy sprinkles

Put the flour and salt in a bowl. Make a well and add the eggs one at a time, beating well after each addition. Add the vanilla and mix until a soft dough forms. On a lightly floured surface, knead the dough, divide it in half, and roll out each half to a 1/4-inch thickness. Cut each half into strips 1/4-inch wide. Using the palms of your hands, roll the strips to the thickness of pencils; cut them into 1/2-inch-long segments. In a skillet of hot oil, fry the pieces one layer deep (do not crowd) until golden brown on all sides. Remove and drain the pieces on paper towels.

Heat the honey and sugar in another skillet over medium heat for 5 minutes. Remove the skillet from the heat and add the deep-fried pieces. Stir until all the pieces are coated with the honey mixture. Remove the pieces with a slotted spoon and let them cool on wax paper. Decorate with sprinkles; break the clusters apart and serve in pieces.

Serves 6 to 8.

Pears Stuffed with Gorgonzola Cheese

    4 fresh pears, peeled, halved,
      and cored
      Lemon juice
    3 ounces Gorgonzola cheese
    3 tablespoons butter
    2/3 cup chopped walnuts or
      pignoli
      Lettuce leaves

Dip the pears in the lemon juice to keep them from turning brown. Cream the Gorgonzola cheese and butter until smooth and creamy. Fill the centers of 4 pear halves with the creamed mixture; then press together with the remaining halves to form "whole" pears. Roll the pears in the nuts and arrange on a lettuce-lined plate. Chill for 1 hour.

Serves 4.

Pears Con Vino

½ cup sugar
½ cup water
1 stick cinnamon
½ cup Italian red wine
2 fresh pears, scrubbed but not peeled
Whipped cream, optional

Bring the sugar, water, cinnamon stick, and wine to a boil; boil for 10 to 12 minutes. Cut the pears in half; remove the cores and seeds. Add the pears to the syrup, lower the heat, and simmer for 15 minutes. Remove the pears to sherbet glasses and pour a little wine syrup over them. Top with whipped cream if desired. Serve hot or cold.

Serves 4.

Zabaione

4 egg yolks, beaten
¼ cup sugar
½ cup Marsala wine
1 teaspoon vanilla extract

Place the egg yolks, sugar, and Marsala in the top of a double boiler that is placed over, not in, boiling water and beat until well blended. Continue to beat the mixture until it is thick, but fluffy. Blend in the vanilla. Serve hot or cold, in stemmed glasses.

Serves 4.

Ricotta Pie

2 cups all-purpose flour
½ teaspoon salt
1 cup lard
2 egg yolks
2 tablespoons cold water

Grease a 9-inch pie plate. Mix together the flour and salt; cut in the lard. Add the egg yolks and water and blend thoroughly. Shape the pastry into a ball and flatten it on a floured surface. Roll out the pastry into a circle with a diameter 1 inch larger than the inverted pie plate. Place the pastry in the plate; pinch the edge of the pastry to stand up ¼ inch above the edge of the plate.

Preheat the oven to 350 degrees.

Prepare the filling and pour it into the pastry-lined pie plate. Bake the pie until the filling is firm, about 1 hour. Cool before serving.

Serves 6 to 8.

Pie Filling

3½ cups ricotta cheese
¼ cup all-purpose flour
1 tablespoon grated orange rind
1 tablespoon grated lemon rind
1 tablespoon vanilla extract
½ teaspoon salt
1 teaspoon cinnamon
4 eggs
1 cup sugar

Mix together the ricotta, flour, orange and lemon rinds, vanilla extract, salt, and cinnamon. Beat the eggs until they are light and foamy. Stir the eggs into the ricotta mixture. Gradually add the sugar until the mixture is well blended.

Frosted Grapes

¼ cup water
¾ cup sugar
1½ pounds seedless grapes

Mix the water and ½ cup of the sugar together in a saucepan; boil for 6 to 7 minutes. Remove the pan from the heat. Dip clusters of the grapes in the syrup; sprinkle with the remaining sugar. Put the coated clusters on a rack until the sugar hardens. Cool and serve.

Rum Balls

2 cups chocolate wafer crumbs
2 cups confectioners' sugar
1 cup ground almonds or pecans
1 cup chopped almonds or pecans
¼ cup cocoa
¼ cup rum (light or dark)
3 tablespoons corn syrup
¼ cup sugar

Combine the wafer crumbs, confectioners' sugar, ground nuts, chopped nuts, and cocoa. Mix thoroughly with your hands. Mix the rum and corn syrup then pour the mixture into the dry ingredients. Blend thoroughly. Pinch off pieces of the dough and roll them into balls the size of walnuts. Then roll the balls in the sugar. Refrigerate the cookies in a tightly covered container for two days before serving.

Makes 4 dozen balls.

Cenci Cookies

2 cups all-purpose flour
2 tablespoons butter
5 tablespoons sugar
3 eggs, beaten
1 teaspoon salt
Grated rind of 1 lemon
3 tablespoons wine (red or white)
Oil for frying
Confectioners' sugar

Put the flour in a bowl and cut in the butter. Add the sugar, eggs, salt, lemon rind, and wine; mix well. Knead the dough thoroughly in the bowl. Cover the bowl with a damp cloth for about 30 minutes. Roll out about ¼ of the dough at a time into an 8-inch-long rectangle and cut each rectangle into about 12 8-by-½-inch strips with a ravioli cutter or knife. Tie each strip into a loose knot. Fry the knots in oil and drain them well on paper towels. Let the cookies cool and sprinkle them with confectioners' sugar.

Makes about 4 dozen cookies.

Almond-Ricotta Cheese Fritters

....

½ pound almond macaroons,
    finely crushed
1 pound ricotta cheese
2 tablespoons sugar
½ teaspoon cinnamon
3 eggs, beaten
1 cup all-purpose flour
1 egg, beaten
2 cups bread crumbs
1½ cups oil
    Confectioners' sugar

Place the macaroons, ricotta, sugar, cinnamon, 3 eggs, and flour in a bowl; mix well. With floured hands, roll the mixture into balls. Dip the balls in the remaining egg and coat with the bread crumbs. Heat the oil in a skillet and fry a few fritters at a time until they are golden brown on all sides. Remove them with a slotted spoon and sprinkle with confectioners' sugar. Serve hot or cold.

Makes 3 or 4 dozen fritters.

Few people know what to do with ricotta cheese, but it's very versatile. Use it in lasagna, manicotti, cannoli, puddings, and pies. Furthermore, it's very good for diets because it has less salt than cottage cheese and is very low in calories. It's also much creamier tasting than cottage cheese.

Anise Cookies

....

4 eggs
1 cup sugar
1 teaspoon vanilla extract
⅓ cup milk
2 tablespoons anise seed
3 cups all-purpose flour
4 teaspoons baking powder
1 cup shortening

Preheat the oven to 375 degrees.

Beat the eggs well. Add the sugar, vanilla extract, milk, and anise seed; mix thoroughly. In another bowl, mix 3 cups of the flour and the baking powder; cut in the shortening. Add the liquid mixture. (You may have to add more flour or milk to achieve a cookie-dough consistency.) Roll out the dough on a lightly floured board and cut it into desired shapes. Bake the pieces on greased cookie sheets for about 12 minutes.

Makes 6 to 8 dozen cookies.

Ricotta Pudding

¾ pound ricotta cheese
¼ cup semisweet chocolate
   chips
¼ cup chopped pecans
3 tablespoons heavy cream
¼ cup raisins
¼ teaspoon cinnamon
2 tablespoons sugar
   Whole pecans for garnish

Cream the ricotta. Add all the other ingredients except the pecans; mix thoroughly. Spoon the mixture into sherbet glasses and chill. Garnish each portion with a whole pecan before serving.

Serves 6.

Banana Fritters

1 cup all-purpose flour
1 teaspoon baking powder
⅛ teaspoon salt
½ cup sugar
2 eggs
½ cup milk
4 or 5 bananas (not too ripe),
   sliced
   Oil for frying
   Confectioners' sugar

Combine the flour, baking powder, salt, sugar, eggs, and milk; mix well. Stir in the sliced bananas. Heat the oil to 375 degrees in a heavy skillet. Drop the batter by tablespoonfuls into the hot oil and fry until the fritters are golden brown on all sides. Remove them and drain on paper towels. Sprinkle the fritters with confectioners' sugar.

Serves 4 to 6.

Ricotta Italian Cream Puffs

1 cup water
½ cup butter
Pinch of salt
1 cup all-purpose flour
4 eggs
Cream Puff Filling (recipe follows)
Confectioners' sugar

Preheat the oven to 400 degrees.

Bring the water to a boil and add the butter and salt; stir over medium heat until the butter is melted. Lower the heat and add the flour, stirring rapidly until the mixture leaves the sides of the pan. Remove the pan from the heat and add the eggs, one at a time, beating after each addition.

Drop the mixture by tablespoonfuls on an ungreased cookie sheet. Bake at 400 degrees for 15 minutes then lower the heat to 350 degrees and bake for 20 minutes more. Remove the puffs to a rack to cool.

Slit the top of the puffs and fill each one with an equal amount of filling. Sprinkle the top of each puff with confectioners' sugar before serving.

Makes 10 to 12 puffs.

Cream Puff Filling

2 cups ricotta cheese
½ cup sugar
1 teaspoon vanilla extract
1 tablespoon cinnamon
2 tablespoons chocolate chips

Mix together all ingredients.

Index